I0438953

Preliminary Surficial Geologic Map of the Newberry Springs 30' x 60' Quadrangle, California

By G.A. Phelps, D.R. Bedford, D.J. Lidke, D.M. Miller, and K.M. Schmidt

Pamphlet to accompany

Open-File Report 2011–1044

2012

U.S. Department of the Interior
U.S. Geological Survey

U.S. Department of the Interior
KEN SALAZAR, Secretary

U.S. Geological Survey
Marcia K. McNutt, Director

U.S. Geological Survey, Reston, Virginia: 2012

For product and ordering information:
World Wide Web: http://www.usgs.gov/pubprod
Telephone: 1–888–ASK–USGS

For more information on the USGS—the Federal source for science about the Earth,
its natural and living resources, natural hazards, and the environment:
World Wide Web: http://www.usgs.gov
Telephone: 1–888–ASK–USGS

Suggested citation:

Phelps, G.A., Bedford, D.R., Lidke, D.J., Miller, D.M., and Schmidt, K.M., 2012, Preliminary surficial geologic
map of the Newberry Springs 30' x 60' quadrangle, California: U.S. Geological Survey Open-File Report
2011–1044, pamphlet 68 p., 1 sheet, scale 1:100,000. (Available at http://pubs.usgs.gov/of/2011/1044/.)

Contents

Figures

Tables

This page intentionally left blank

Preliminary Surficial Geologic Map of the Newberry Springs 30' x 60' Quadrangle, California

By G.A. Phelps, D.R. Bedford, D.J. Lidke, D.M. Miller, and K.M. Schmidt

Introduction

The Newberry Springs 30' x 60' quadrangle is located in the central Mojave Desert of southern California. It is split approximately into northern and southern halves by I-40, with the city of Barstow at its western edge and the town of Ludlow near its eastern edge. The map area spans lat 34°30' to 35° N. to long –116° to –117° W. and covers over 1,000 km^2. We integrate the results of surficial geologic mapping conducted during 2002–2005 with compilations of previous surficial mapping and bedrock geologic mapping. Quaternary units are subdivided in detail on the map to distinguish variations in age, process of formation, pedogenesis, lithology, and spatial interdependency, whereas pre-Quaternary bedrock units are grouped into generalized assemblages that emphasize their attributes as hillslope-forming materials and sources of parent material for the Quaternary units.

The spatial information in this publication is presented in two forms: a spatial database and a geologic map. The geologic map is a *view* (the display of an extracted subset of the database at a given time) of the spatial database; it highlights key aspects of the database and necessarily does not show all of the data contained therein. The database contains detailed information about Quaternary geologic unit composition, authorship, and notes regarding geologic units, faults, contacts, and local vegetation. The amount of information contained in the database is too large to show on a single map, so a restricted subset of the information was chosen to summarize the overall nature of the geology. Refer to the database for additional information.

Accompanying the spatial data are the map documentation and spatial metadata. The map documentation (this document) describes the geologic setting and history of the Newberry Springs map sheet, summarizes the age and physical character of each map unit, and describes principal faults and folds. The Federal Geographic Data Committee (FGDC) compliant metadata provides detailed information about the digital files and file structure of the spatial data.

Physiographic Setting

The Newberry Springs 30' x 60' quadrangle in the central and eastern Mojave Desert of Southern California (fig. 1) contains several mountain ranges including, from east to west, the Bristol, Cady, Bullion, Lava Bed, Rodman, Fry, Newberry, Calico, and Ord Mountains (fig. 2). The ephemeral Mojave River flows through the northwestern part of the map area. Its headwaters lie in the San Bernardino Mountains southwest of the Newberry Springs map area and its terminus is Silver Lake, east of the map area and just north of the town of Baker, California. Piedmont alluvial plains dominate much of the landscape and locally terminate downhill at the base of the closed basins of Broadwell, Lavic, Troy, Galway, and Lucerne (northern end) dry lakes. The Newberry Springs map area contains three cinder cones and associated basaltic lava fields, both probably Quaternary in age: Pisgah Crater, Sunshine Crater, and an unnamed crater in the Newberry mountains. The lava flows from these craters are prominent features in the central portion of the map.

1

Elevations in the map area range from a low of less than 300 m near the southeast corner of the quadrangle to a high of almost 2,000 m at Ord Mountain. The climate is arid to semi-arid. The mean annual temperature at Barstow, estimated from NOAA climate normals for the U.S., 1951–1980 (Stoffer, 2004), is about 65°, with a mean annual high of 80° and a mean annual low of 48°. The mean annual precipitation is approximately 4 inches.

The map area is part of the tectonically active Mojave Desert Block of Dokka and Travis (1990) and contains numerous faults active during the Quaternary. The geologic structure is dominated by steeply dipping, northwest-striking faults that have accommodated considerable amounts of right-lateral strike-slip motion during the late Cenozoic. Along with the San Andreas Fault west of the map area, these faults form part of the broad and structurally complex Pacific-North American transform boundary (Garfunkel, 1974; Dokka and Travis, 1990; Atwater, 1992). Dokka and Travis named the Mojave Desert Block and Death Valley region as the Eastern California Shear Zone, which they consider to have absorbed 65–80 km of right-lateral shear strain since the middle Miocene (Dokka and Travis, 1990).

The central part of the map area is traversed by the Barstow-Bristol trough, a major structural depression trending west-northwest (Gardner, 1940). The deepest Cenozoic sedimentary basin in the quadrangle, which is centered near Barstow, is as much as 3 km deep, based on gravity- inversion modeling (Jachens and others, 2002). The second deepest sedimentary basin in the area is centered over the piedmont alluvial fans and hills of the Bristol Mountains southeast of Broadwell Lake; this basin is notable for being offset from the current topographic basin in this area. Except for the Pisgah and Calico Faults, the northwest-striking faults of the Eastern California Shear Zone cannot be traced through the Barstow-Bristol Trough. This suggests that the Barstow-Bristol Trough is a major crustal structure (Miller and others, 1982).

Several previous works have summarized the pre-Quaternary geologic history of parts of the map area (Gardner, 1940; Bishop, 1963; Bassett and Kupfer, 1964; Miller and others, 1982; Dokka, 1983; Dokka and Travis, 1990; Miller and others, 1991; Glazner and others, 2000; Glazner and others, 2002), including the following major events: (1) Deposition, intrusion, and metamorphism of Proterozoic rocks was followed by uplift and erosion and, in turn, by unconformable deposition of Cambrian through Permian miogeoclinal sediments. (2) Intrusion of Jurassic and Cretaceous plutons was accompanied by westward-directed folding and faulting. (3) Additional crustal deformation likely occurred prior to late Cretaceous plutonism, although timing of this episode of Cordilleran thrusting is ambiguous. (4) Deposition of early Miocene volcanic rocks coincided with detachment faulting that extended the Earth's crust in this region and tilted the early Miocene and older units. (5) Extension was followed in late early Miocene by fluvial and lacustrine sedimentation in supradetachment basins and by occasional volcanism, including that which produced the regionally significant Peach Springs Tuff. (6) Coarse-grained clastic sedimentation resumed in the late Tertiary, as evidenced by widespread thick sequences of alluvial gravels of apparent late Miocene and Pliocene age.

Previous Quaternary Mapping

Previous regional geologic mapping in the quadrangle was completed by Dibblee (15′quadrangles; 1964a,b, 1966, 1967a,b, 1970), Dibblee and Bassett (1966a,b), and Bassett and Kupfer (1964). While these maps do not focus on the Quaternary, they offer the most recent work for much of the Newberry Springs quadrangle area.

Detailed mapping of the Tertiary strata in the northern Bristol Mountains (Brady, 1992) included careful delineation of Quaternary faults.

Casey (1981) mapped the central Bristol Mountains, focusing on the Tertiary volcanic section. He also investigated history of faulting, concluding that all faults within his study area are pre-Quaternary.

This map follows several studies (Dokka, 1983; Cox and others, 1987; Bezore and Pridmore, 1999) that describe the geology of the Newberry and Rodman Mountains. Cox and Wilshire (1993, 1994) provided detailed surficial geologic maps of the Nebo and Yermo Annexes of the Marine Corps Logistics Base, a part of the Mojave River plain east of Barstow. McGill and others (1988) published a detailed map of deformed beds of Lake Manix along the Manix Fault.

Wise (1966) produced detailed maps of volcanic deposits near Pisgah Crater and Sunshine Peak. Basalt flows near Pisgah Crater were dated by Phillips (2003).

Thompson (1929) showed the importance of many northwest-striking faults as barriers to groundwater flow in his excellent description of the geomorphology and groundwater hydrology of the Mojave Desert.

The Quaternary sediments and desiccation cracks at Broadwell Lake were studied extensively by the consulting firms EMCON Associates (1993) and Rasmussen and Associates (1990) as part of a feasibility study for locating a hazardous waste facility.

Numerous publications have outlined the history of Lake Manix and the Mojave River. These studies are described in a following section on this subject. Similarly, detailed fault studies are described in the section on Quaternary faults.

Tectonic Setting

The Newberry Springs quadrangle is located in the Mojave Desert Block, a structural boundary bounded by the San Andreas, Garlock, Pinto Mountain, and Granite Mountains Faults (Dokka and Travis, 1990). Several important Quaternary faults pass through the Newberry Springs quadrangle, including the inactive South Bristol Mountains, Broadwell Lake, Ludlow, Rodman, Pisgah, Cady, Tin Can Alley, Dolores Lake, and Harper Lake Faults, and the active Manix, Calico, West Calico, Bullion, Emerson, Lavic Lake, Lenwood, Homestead Valley, Johnson Valley, and Camp Rock Faults (fig. 3).

Quaternary faults in the map area have two main orientations: northwest-striking and east-striking. Northwest-striking faults include the Calico, Camp Rock, Rodman, Bullion, Lenwood, Ludlow, and Broadwell Lake Faults. East-striking faults include the Manix, Cady, and Broadwell Mesa Faults. Although most faults strike northwest or east, other orientations are observed. North-striking faults occur in the northeast Cady and northwest Bristol Mountains and east of Troy Lake in the western Cady Mountains. Also, the Dolores Lake and Tin Can Alley Faults, in the northwest corner of the map area, strike just west of north.

Two dominant tectonic models have been proposed to explain late Cenozoic faulting in the Mojave Desert Block: one invokes simple shear, and the other splits the Mojave Desert Block into separate kinematic domains. Simple shear models include those proposed by Garfunkel (1974), Carter and others (1987), and Ron and others (2001).

According to Garfunkel (1974), the Mojave Block is the result of accommodating the primary motion of right-lateral shear associated with the San Andreas Fault and the secondary motion of extension in the Basin and Range Province and Continental Borderland. According to this model, the Mojave Block is subject to homogeneous strain, causing northwest-striking faults and neighboring blocks to rotate counterclockwise, superficially like a stack of books tilting on a shelf. This rotation produces left-lateral shear along the north boundary of the Mojave Block, creating the Garlock Fault, a bend in the San Andreas Fault, the provinces of rotated right-lateral northwest-striking faults, and a slight clockwise rotation along left-lateral east-striking faults. The

Sierra Nevada is a fixed structural buttress in this model, against which the Mojave Block shears and rotates. Garfunkel noted that deviations from the model might occur due to irregularities in the upper crust. Allowing for such deviations from perfect homogeneous strain makes the model more broadly applicable, but it also makes the model more difficult to test, because a negative result is poorly defined.

Garfunkel's model is attractive in several respects. First, it explains the simultaneous right-lateral movement along northwest-striking faults in the Mojave Block and left-lateral movement on the adjacent Garlock Fault with one model. Second, it explains the bend in the San Andreas Fault. Third, it is comprehensive in that rotation is summarized by two parameters: the ratio of fault slip to distance between faults and the amount of overall rotation for the block. Fourth, it is quantitative and testable; paleomagnetic data can be used to estimate the amount of overall rotation, which in turn can be used to solve for the ratio of fault slip to the distance between faults. Garfunkel suggested an overall rotation of up to 30° and an aggregate right-lateral displacement of up to 100 km across the block.

Carter and others (1987) built upon the work of Garfunkel (1974) and proposed a model of simple shear, where the northeastern and southeastern parts of the Mojave Desert Block experience east-striking left-lateral shear, and the rest of the block experiences northwest-striking right-lateral shear. Using paleomagnetic data from the eastern Transverse Ranges, they concluded that approximately 40° of clockwise rotation has occurred since the late Miocene in blocks adjacent to left-slip faults. They observed approximately 50 km of left slip along east-striking faults in the area, which implies roughly 100 km of dextral shear distributed across the Mojave Desert Block.

Ron and others (2001) proposed a simple-shear model under a stress regime that rotates through time, with domain rotations similar to those of Carter and others (1987). They described a two-stage model of simple shear, where slip occurs on an older, rotated set of conjugate faults due to the sustained planes of weakness that they define and on a new set of conjugate faults optimally oriented with respect to the modern stress regime of the Mojave Desert Block. The older conjugate faults are currently unfavorably oriented with respect to the modern stress regime due to both fault rotation and the change in the orientation of the maximum stress through time. Evidence of rotation from Carter and others (1987) supports the hypothesis that the stress regime changes direction through time, because paleomagnetic data indicate that the northeastern Mojave and Eastern Transverse Ranges domains (dominated by east-striking left-lateral faults) rotated clockwise, whereas the Central and Western Mojave Blocks (dominated by northwest-striking, right-lateral faults) have not rotated appreciably. The asymmetrical rotation of east-striking and northwest-striking faults can be explained if the stress regime is allowed to change over time. This model was used to explain the multiple surface ruptures along faults of various orientations, observed following the 1992 Landers, Joshua Tree, and Big Bear earthquakes and the 1999 Hector Mine earthquake, by invoking failure on conjugate sets of faults on both the older, rotated faults of the previous stress regime and the newly formed and as yet unrotated faults created under the current stress regime.

Models invoking simple shear explain the overall fault pattern concisely and are roughly consistent with recent tectonic events. One criticism of the simple-shear models, however, is that they predict homogeneous strain throughout the Mojave Desert Block. Previously mapped faults seem to show preferential domains of optimal faulting, indicating that the stress patterns, or at least the response to them, is *not* consistent across the Mojave Desert Block. The observed inhomogeneous strain patterns seem to require a yet more complicated model.

Dokka and Travis (1990) proposed an empirical model to explain the tectonic activity in the Mojave Desert. They argued that the observed slip accumulated along major faults in the Mojave Desert Block is far less than is required by the Garfunkel model. Moreover, they concluded that faulting throughout the Mojave Desert Block is heterogeneous, and they divided the Mojave Desert Block into six subregions of homogenous strain. These subregions are bounded on the east by a major northwest-striking fault that runs from Death Valley south through the Bristol Mountains. They further proposed, based on modern seismicity and stress regime data and on the timing of fault displacements, that the northwest-striking zone of active faulting has shifted westward since its initiation in the Miocene. In their model, the central Mojave Desert Block is now the focus of modern faulting and seismicity.

This model is difficult to test, because any anomalous strain patterns within a subregion can be explained by further subdivision. In this sense, the model is *descriptive* rather than *prescriptive*. Also, total offset is not yet well determined for many of the faults and does not constrain the model. For example, Brady (1992) concludes from local geologic relations that the 21.5-km right-slip displacement on the Granite Mountains Fault suggested by Dokka and Travis (1990) is greatly overestimated. Recent surface ruptures along faults in the central Mojave Desert associated with the Landers and Hector Mine earthquakes support the claim that the central Mojave Desert Block is currently active and, thus, is an important focus of regional deformation, though not necessarily the only such focus.

Our work in the Newberry Springs 30′ x 60′ quadrangle reveals a complex, interrelated pattern of northwest-, north-northwest-, and east-striking faults. Several of the northwest-striking faults (Ludlow, Pisgah, Lavic Lake Faults) change strike northward from northwest to north-northwest as they near about lat 34° 45 N. We found a larger number of east-striking faults than previously mapped, many of which appear to merge complexly with north-northwest- or northwest-striking faults. Interactions between east-striking faults and northerly-striking faults are not typically exposed, and the sequence of faulting is therefore ambiguous. However, an east-striking fault (Manix Fault) and a northerly-striking fault (Lavic Lake Fault) both ruptured in the 20th Century, indicating that strain is currently being accommodated in both directions. We provisionally conclude that, in the Newberry Springs 30′ x 60′ quadrangle, faults do not form discrete domains characterized by a single fault orientation. Rather, stress is being accommodated by faults of multiple orientations. Future tectonic models of the Mojave Desert region must include these more complex fault interactions.

Quaternary Faults

This section describes the age, recurrence interval, and displacement of faults within the Newberry Springs quadrangle that we have identified as Quaternary or probably Quaternary in age. We used a combination of field mapping and aerial photograph interpretation to look for evidence of Quaternary fault rupture. Evidence included offset of geomorphic features such as streams or ridges, fault scarps cutting Quaternary units, deformed Quaternary units, and lithologic changes. Recent ruptures along parts of the Bullion and Pisgah Faults associated with the Landers and Hector Mine earthquakes demonstrate that active faulting can occur simultaneously on multiple neighboring fault traces.

South Bristol Mountains Fault

The South Bristol Mountains Fault is a northwest-trending fault that lies east of the Newberry Springs quadrangle for most of its length, where it was partially mapped by Bassett and Kupfer (1964), and later described by Miller and others (1982), and Bedford and others (2006).

In the Amboy 30′ x 60′ quadrangle, east of, and adjacent to, the Newberry Springs quadrangle, the South Bristol Mountains Fault cuts late Pleistocene alluvial fan deposits (unit

Qiao) in several places on the southwest side of the South Bristol Mountains, but farther northwest it lies within bedrock and does not unambiguously cut Quaternary deposits.

The fault continues into the Bristol Mountains area of the Newberry Springs quadrangle, where it is less distinct than in many areas to the east, and has few geomorphic features associated with it. We have not directly studied the fault within the Newberry Springs quadrangle, but its trace is extended from the mapped trace in the Amboy quadrangle along a linear zone of disrupted Miocene strata. The fault appears to die out to the northwest before reaching Broadwell Valley.

Broadwell Lake Fault

The Broadwell Lake Fault was first described by Ford and others (1990). They identified the fault on processed Landsat Thematic Mapper images that show a lithologic contrast between discontinuous exposures of tuff and tuff breccia. Our studies in the adjacent Amboy quadrangle indicate that the fault is exposed discontinuously and apparently has not been active since the Pleistocene, because it does not cut alluvial deposits of late Pleistocene (Qiay) or early Holocene age (Bedford and others, 2006). In the Newberry Springs quadrangle we mapped two strands of the fault where aerial photographs and field observations revealed low scarps and ridges crossing Pleistocene alluvial deposits with pronounced desert pavements (Qiao). Fieldwork did not reveal prominent fault scarps, however, or indication of more recent movement on the fault. This evidence suggests that the fault was active in the early to middle Pleistocene, in agreement with the previous interpretation by Ford and others (1990).

Broadwell Mesa Fault

The Broadwell Mesa Fault is a newly mapped east-striking fault that cuts units Qiao and mv across Broadwell Mesa in the west Bristol Mountains. To the east, the fault is untraceable as it crosses into grus-dominated alluvial sediments, and, to the west, it is untraceable across alluvium and bedrock units of the northwestern Bristol Mountains. The fault is co-linear with the Cady Fault to the west, but we found no evidence of a connection between the two faults.

Ludlow Fault

The Ludlow Fault was mapped previously by Kupfer and Bassett (1962), Bassett and Kupfer (1964), and Dibblee (1967a, b). As mapped by Kupfer and Bassett (1962), the fault extends from Lead Mountain, just west of Bristol lake, northwestward to the town of Ludlow, California. As mapped by Dibblee, the fault extends over 65 km, trending northwest of Bristol Lake, then bending north near the town of Ludlow, and finally bending back to the northwest just north of Broadwell Lake. Howard and Miller (1992) studied the southern end of the fault in the Parker 30' x 60' quadrangle. They inferred at least 6 km of dextral displacement by relating clasts in a dipping conglomerate unit east of the fault to source rocks west of the fault. They restrict the age of the most recent fault activity to middle Pleistocene or older by noting that the fault does not cut a Quaternary unit containing basalt clasts derived from Lead Mountain; basalt bedrock at Lead Mountain has been dated at 360 ka by the K-Ar whole rock method. In the map area the fault produces several prominent geomorphic features that allow it to be traced, somewhat discontinuously, along most of its mapped extent.

The Ludlow Fault enters the map area near its southeast corner. Here the fault is exposed at several neighboring locations, where it cuts partly consolidated late Tertiary to early Quaternary sediments and appears to truncate desert pavements, generating a prominent northwest-trending, down-to-the-west, line of low hills. These hills are approximately perpendicular to the alluvial fan gradient and disrupt the drainage in this part of the fan (fig. 4). Farther northwest, continuing along trend, late Pleistocene to early Holocene alluvial fan deposits (Qyao) are slightly elevated on the east side of the fault for another 3.5 km. Ten kilometers farther northwest, near the gas line road, the Ludlow Fault is exposed in several outcrops, one clearly cutting a late Pleistocene pavement (fig. 4). There is more than one mappable strand in this area. The fault can be traced from geomorphic expression through the mountains south of Ludlow, where it continues to exhibit multiple strands. Kupfer and Bassett (1962) also noted multiple strands of the Ludlow fault in this area, whereas Dibblee (1967a) mapped a single through-going fault.

North of Ludlow, it is not clear if the fault continues as a single fault or zone or if it merges with other faults. Along strike to the northwest there is geomorphic evidence of a northwest-trending fault near the east tip of the Sleeping Beauty Mountains, but the evidence is subtle and restricted to a small area. More persuasive geomorphic evidence exists north-northwest of Ludlow, where a linear series of low, truncated hills (Qha/mv) at the southeast end of the Cady Mountains appears to be uplifted relative to adjacent Quaternary units. Similar to the deposits to the south, the linear series of hills is perpendicular to alluvial fan gradient and down to the west and here exposes Tertiary volcanic rocks. There is no clear evidence that adjoining Quaternary deposits are faulted. Jachens and others (2002) interpreted offset magnetic anomalies to trace several faults in the Central Mojave and measure their lateral displacements. For this portion of the Ludlow Fault, their interpretation agrees with the mapping of Dibblee (1967b) and Bassett and Kupfer (1964), who traced the Ludlow Fault into the alluvium north of the linear series of low hills. This latter part of the fault trace skirts the edge of the magnetic data, however, and is therefore poorly constrained by this evidence. Jachens and others (2002) estimate that 12 km of right-lateral displacement has occurred across the fault, based on the offset of prominent magnetic anomalies.

Beyond the linear series of low hills, the fault may either die out along strike to the north-northwest or continue almost due north along the west side of Broadwell Lake onward to the eastern front of the Cady Mountains, as mapped by Dibblee (1967b), Bassett and Kupfer (1964), and Jachens and others (2002). There is evidence of a Quaternary fault scarp along the mountain front, which vertically offsets Quaternary boulder debris-flow deposits as much as 2 m down to the east. Farther north, the mountain front bends to the northwest and is bordered by abundant evidence of faulting in the form of truncated hillslopes. Field evidence of a fault cutting Pleistocene desert-pavement deposits indicates that faulting occurred since the middle to late Pleistocene.

There is abundant evidence that the Ludlow Fault was active during the middle to late Pleistocene. There is no evidence of more recent activity, although fault scarps tend to be poorly preserved in units of latest Pleistocene to Holocene alluvial deposits. The northern extension of the fault beyond the southeastern Cady Mountains is ambiguous and, consequently, is not shown on this map. The Lavic Lake Fault follows a sinuous path, northwest to north then northwest again, and this pattern could be repeated for the Ludlow Fault. Alternatively, the northern trace of the fault as previously mapped might consist of several independent faults, some trending north and others northwest. Careful mapping at 1:24,000, accompanied by further geophysical investigations, would likely clarify these ambiguous structural relations.

Lavic Lake Fault

The Lavic Lake Fault, as mapped by Dibblee (1966), branches northward from the Bullion Fault just south of the Newberry Springs 30′ x 60′ quadrangle. As it exits the north end of the Bullion Mountains it bends to the northwest, where Dibblee shows the fault disappearing beneath Quaternary alluvial fan deposits. The Lavic Lake Fault was one of five faults that ruptured during the 1999 M_w 7.1 Hector Mine earthquake (the fault was unnamed prior to the earthquake; Treiman and others, 2002). The rupture on the Lavic Lake Fault extended northwest beyond the previously mapped termination, striking northwest to the west edge of Lavic Lake playa and then curving northward into the Pisgah Lava Flow. The continuous trace of the fault terminates just beyond the southern edge of the flow. Minor ruptures occurred to the north and northwest, including ruptures along the east side of the Pisgah Cinder Cone (Sylvester and others, 2002; Treiman and others, 2002) and on an unnamed, north-trending fault that initiates approximately 2 km west of the Pisgah Cinder Cone. The surface rupture consisted of many small, left-stepping, en echelon strands, often linked by small bends and associated areas of local compressional uplift. At the zone of rupture, the maximum displacement for the Hector Mine earthquake was roughly 5 m. The mapped trace recorded in this database was generalized from Treiman and others (2002).

Rymer and others (2002) came to several conclusions on the history of the Lavic Lake Fault, based on trench studies across the fault after the Hector Mine earthquake. First, no evidence of previous faulting prior to the Hector Mine earthquake could be found in three trenches dug across the surface rupture. The sediments in the trenches are estimated to span the past 7 ka. It is, therefore, possible that the 1999 surface rupture followed a new route north of the Bullion Mountains. However, Rymer and others (2002) did find evidence of an older rupture, dated approximately 260 AD in a trench across a nearby vegetation lineament, which shows that the general zone did exist prior to 1999 and was active in the recent past.

Our field photos record the rupture trace in 2005, 6 years after the Hector Mine earthquake (fig. 5). Many of the fractures on the playa have already begun to fill with sediment and have established vegetation. However, many other fractures are still quite prominent. In the playa fringe—distal alluvial fan deposits south of Lavic Lake—local geomorphic ridges and sags can still be distinguished, but are rapidly succumbing to erosion.

The Lavic Lake Fault is an active fault. It is interesting to note that on a large scale the Hector Mine surface rupture stepped right across five faults but locally stepped left along the Lavic Lake Fault.

Bullion Fault

The Bullion Fault is a prominent northwest-striking fault that extends into the map area from the south. Its trace in the map area was mapped from field observations and aerial photography. The north strand of the Bullion Fault, present in the map area, did not rupture in the 1999 Hector Mine earthquake. Slip was instead transferred northward onto the Lavic Lake Fault just south of the map area.

The Bullion Fault has pronounced geomorphic and structural expression along the southwest edge of the Bullion Mountains; steep linear range front, fault scarps cutting desert pavements, and juxtaposition of contrasting bedrock units clearly mark the location of the fault. However, a more complex fault pattern emerges at the north end of the Bullion Mountains. A parallel fault that appears ~2 km to the southwest of the main strand may represent a left step in the Bullion Fault that connects northwestward with the Rodman Fault. Prominent fault scarps cut late Pleistocene desert pavements—and possibly early Holocene deposits—along this fault, indicating an age similar to that of the main strand. A second fault either splays or steps northeastward, apparently linking with the Pisgah Fault, although the exact nature of the connection is concealed beneath Holocene and latest Pleistocene alluvium.

Evidence of compressional deformation is found near the north end of the Bullion Fault, just southeast of the Rodman and Pisgah Faults. A zone of splaying or en echelon faulting is observed between the Bullion Fault and the West Calico Fault. Here, Tertiary and early Quaternary sedimentary and volcanic units are strongly uplifted between the Bullion and West Calico Faults, forming a major topographic divide between southward- and northward-flowing streams. Just southeast of the drainage divide late Pleistocene alluvial fan deposits (Qiay) are tilted east northeast as steeply as 9°. This suggests significant compression, and related folding and tectonic uplift, has occurred since the Late Pleistocene.

Cady Fault

The Cady Fault is an oblique left-lateral feature, striking roughly east-west, with a length of ~20 km. It terminates abruptly to the east where it intersects a spur of the Cady Mountains near Hidden Valley. Its west end is either (1) concealed by young and active eolian deposits south of the Mojave River and, hence, likely continues farther west in the subsurface or (2) it might terminate against a concealed northward extension of the Rodman Fault. Recently acquired, unpublished ground and aeromagnetic data depict patterns that support the interpretation that the Cady Fault extends westward into the eolian dominated deposits but that it changes orientation to a more northwesterly strike. It was first mapped by Kupfer and Bassett (1962) and Dibblee and Bassett (1966a), later included in a regional compilation by Rogers (1967), recognized using remote sensing by Ford and others (1990), and included in the state fault compilation by Jennings (1994). A south-side-up relation exists for both Miocene volcanic and granitic bedrock, as well as younger and older Pleistocene units (Qia and Qoa), which is consistent with progressive up-to-the-south oblique slip. The youngest units definitely displaced by faulting are late Pleistocene in age (Qiay), while some smaller early Holocene units (Qyao) may have been displaced or deposited in response to earlier displacement. The Cady Fault is colinear with the Broadwell Mesa Fault to the east, but we found no evidence of a connection between the faults.

West Calico Fault

From its northern terminus in the Rodman Mountains, the West Calico Fault parallels the Calico Fault southeastward to the Lava Bed Mountains, where the latter dies out in a series of complex splays. The West Calico Fault also manifests as a series of splays as it traverses the northeast end of Iron Ridge. Dibblee (1966) mapped a continuous strand of the West Calico Fault that continues southeast, concealed beneath the alluvium, before becoming visible in outcrop along the southwest edge of the Bullion Mountains. We have not mapped this concealed strand, because it is not clear if the West Calico Fault continues southeast of Iron Ridge as one single strand, several splays that die out, or if the fault steps to the right. The fault defines the southwest edge of the Bullion Mountains as it continues southeastward to the south margin of the Newberry Springs quadrangle.

The West Calico Fault is prominently exposed along the southwest edge of the Lava Bed Mountains, where it is expressed by fault scarps in desert pavements, shutter ridges, and a steep, linear mountain front. Fault strands are locally expressed in partially consolidated alluvium of latest Tertiary to Quaternary age in a wash 1.5 km southeast of Maumee Mine. In the western Bullion Mountains, fault scarps mapped from areal photographs cut middle Pleistocene to late Holocene pavements (Qiao) and possibly cut one late Pleistocene to early Holocene geomorphic surface (Qyao).

Pisgah Fault

The Pisgah Fault initiates north of the Bullion Fault in the Bullion Mountains south of Lavic Lake (figs. 2, 3), strikes north-northwest, then cuts both the basaltic flows of Sunshine Peak and the Pisgah basalt flows before being concealed by eolian deposits just north of I-40. Where the fault cuts Sunshine Peak, an approximately 100-m, down-to-the-east vertical topographic escarpment is present. Ross (1992) studied the southwest Cady Mountains, which, according to his paleomagnetic data, have rotated clockwise ~83° since ~16 ma. He attributes the rotation to dextral shearing of the southwestern Cady Mountains Block between the Pisgah and Rodman Faults. Using the methods of Mckenzie and Jackson (1983), Ross infers that 15±4 km of slip has occurred on the Pisgah-Rodman Fault system to account for the rotation of the southwestern Cady Mountains Block. This is in rough agreement with the 6.3 km of slip suggested for the Pisgah Fault based on the alignment of magnetic anomalies (Jachens and others, 2002), combined with a possible 20 km total offset on the Bullion-Pisgah-Rodman Fault System. This result would imply roughly 14 km of slip on the Bullion-Rodman Fault System and between 5 and 13 km of slip on the Rodman Fault.

The Pisgah Fault cuts the western part of the Pisgah Field and, therefore, the latest activity on the fault is no older than about 20 ka (see section on Quaternary Volcanic Rocks).

Manix Fault

The Manix Fault, as mapped by Dibblee and Bassett (1966a), Keaton and Keaton (1977), and McGill and others (1988), was first studied by Richter (1947) following the Manix earthquake of 1947. Richter demonstrated that the nearly east-striking fault generated about 2–3 cm of sinistral offset across the surface rupture trace. McGill and others (1988) mapped in detail a part of the fault near Manix Wash, where it cuts Pleistocene Lake Manix deposits and forms steep folds in deposits ranging in age from late Pliocene and early Pleistocene (QTop) to late Pleistocene. We traced strath terrace deposits created by an abandoned meander of the ancestral Mojave River to the area of Manix Wash, and found no evidence that they were cut by a fault, despite the fact that the 1947 earthquake ruptured through this area. The strath deposits overlie and, thus, must have formed after, member D of the Manix formation of Jefferson (2003), which was assigned a latest Pleistocene age (~70 to 20 ka) by Jefferson (2003). This observation provides a cautionary tale for those attempting to date faults without trenching: some Holocene materials may not be sufficiently cohesive to preserve small fault scarps for longer than a few decades.

The Manix Fault cannot be conclusively identified along the Mojave River plain west of Manix Wash, but several subtle geomorphic lineaments may mark the fault in this area, and these features are identified in the map database. South of Harvard Hill, several exposed east-striking faults place Pleistocene Lake Manix deposits on the south against Miocene strata, and a few Pleistocene alluvial fan deposits (Qiay) are cut by structurally analogous, south-facing scarps. In one place, fan deposits of Pleistocene to Holocene age (Qyao) are clearly cut by a scarp, verifying a Holocene age for the western part of the Manix Fault. Others have mapped the Manix Fault as cutting through Harvard Hill, where different Miocene strata are juxtaposed, but we found no definite evidence for Quaternary offset on that strand. The Manix Fault projects westward from Harvard Hill and aligns with several linear terraces and channel margins north of the Mojave River, but we found no definitive exposures in Quaternary deposits west of Harvard Hill. Farther west, the projection of the Manix Fault intersects I–15 at the south edge of the locally named Toomey Hills. In the freeway roadcut, only small faults are exposed, but folded Miocene, Pliocene, and Pleistocene strata indicate youthful deformation. At the west end of the Toomey Hills, a scarp cuts Pleistocene (Qia) deposits and Lake Manix deposits (Qil), and this fault has been interpreted as the Manix Fault by Meek (1990).

East of Manix Wash the Manix Fault cuts Pliocene fanglomerate and Pliocene to early Pleistocene playa deposits of the Mojave River formation as far east as Afton Canyon (Keaton and Keaton, 1977). Meek and Battles (1991) determined a minimum left-lateral offset of 5.2 km for the fault based on an apparent offset of distinctive Tertiary fanglomerate(?) directly north of the map area. Total offset based on older markers has not been established. Along Manix Wash and to the east along Buwalda Ridge, Tertiary fanglomerate, Pliocene to early Pleistocene playa and alluvial deposits (QTop), and Pleistocene Lake Manix beds (Qil) are cut and deformed by strands of the Manix Fault. Within this region, McGill and others (1988) mapped a narrow band of broad, northeast-trending folds along the south side of the strand of the Manix Fault that ruptured during the 1947 earthquake, and they noted that these folds deform the Pliocene to early Pleistocene beds (QTop) and the middle to late Pleistocene Lake Manix beds. The orientation of these folds relative to the Manix Fault implies either a small component of right-lateral shear or pure fault-normal compression (McGill and others, 1988). However, the evidence for 5 cm of left-lateral slip following the 1947 Manix earthquake (Buwalda and Richter, 1948) and evidence for several kilometers of left-lateral offset of a distinctive Tertiary fanglomerate in the Cady Mountains to the northeast (Meek and Battles, 1991), suggest that both historical and long-term lateral displacement has been dominated by left-lateral slip. This short- and long-term evidence for left-lateral slip might then imply that a north-south oriented component of compression is principally responsible for the formation of the narrow band of northeast-trending folds near Manix Wash and Buwalda Ridge.

Calico Fault

The Calico Fault, as mapped by McCulloh (1965), Dibblee (1964a, 1966, 1970), Dibblee and Bassett (1966b), and Cox (in press), strikes northwest and locally consists of two parallel strands southeast of Newberry Springs. Southward, the fault cuts obliquely across mountainous terrane and, northward, it crosses the broad lowlands of the Mojave River plain and then swerves westward along the southern front of the Calico Mountains.

The northern reach of the fault consists of two to three splays in most cases, each cutting Pleistocene deposits of diverse ages and origins, and many cutting Holocene deposits. In the piedmont southeast of Newberry Springs, the ages of alluvial fan deposits are distinguish by characteristic soils and vegetation. The deposits are very late Pleistocene to middle Holocene, although the best exposed deposits (Qyao) bracket the Pleistocene-Holocene boundary and are cut by fault scarps that drop the land surface ≤1m down to the northeast. At right bends and steps in the fault, several scarps of 3.4 m can be identified that cumulatively offset Qyao surfaces. Middle Holocene deposits (Qyay) are probably cut in several places by fault scarps, but the geomorphic evidence of faulting is generally ambiguous. North of Newberry Springs, the fault consists of two strands that step left in two places. Scarps display down-to-the-northeast morphology. One splay of the Calico Fault observed in outcrop near the south bank of the Mojave River consists of two parallel, nearly vertical (strike 325°, dip 87° NE.) faults with associated fissure fills. Near the north bank of the Mojave River, fluvial deposits of middle or late Holocene age (Qaw or Qywy) are cut by scarps as high as 1.2 m, and Pleistocene-Holocene boundary deposits (Qywo) appear to be offset dextrally 25 to 30 m. North of the river, Pleistocene Mojave River gravels are uplifted in a series of benches that outline several splays of the Calico Fault that appear to coalesce in a hill and associated southwest-dipping thrust faults immediately south of the I-15 freeway. This hill may represent the site where the Calico Fault enters a major restraining bend approaching the front of the Calico Mountains. This site also approximately coincides with the westward projection of known traces of the Manix Fault and the southward projection of the Tin Can Alley Fault (Dudash, 2006). We have not found exposures of the Manix or Tin Can Alley Faults near this hill that would help to clarify the geometry or history of faulting.

The Calico Fault along the southern front of the Calico Mountains is quite unlike segments farther southeast. Here it strikes west-northwest, oblique to the neighboring segments (McCulloh, 1965); it appears to accommodate tens to hundreds of meters of down-to-the-south offset, and it can be shown to cut alluvial deposits no younger than early late Pleistocene (Qiao). This segment of the fault has been interpreted as a restraining bend, and the relief of the adjacent Calico Mountains was caused by a component of thrusting or other contractile processes (Oskin and Iriondo, 2004). Our studies identified two new features. First, two east-striking faults were observed within metavolcanic rocks at the southeast tip of the Calico Mountains. These faults have subhorizontal striations and project eastward toward another east-striking fault that cuts late Pleistocene (Qiay) deposits. Although these east-striking faults all lie south of the Calico Fault, they are approximately aligned with the western part of the Manix Fault. Second, in several places alluvial fans shed from the Calico Mountains contain small scarps representing faulting southwest of the main Calico Fault Zone. Most scarps cut late Pleistocene (Qiay) deposits but not younger deposits; however, one scarp near the southeast end of the Calico Mountains cuts latest Pleistocene deposits (young Qiay) and associated soils that are probably 25 to 30 ka based on pedological dating of similar soils elsewhere. These relations suggest that major activity of the more northerly segments of the Calico Fault Zone ceased during the early late Pleistocene but that minor activity continued into the very late Pleistocene along splays that stepped southward from the main fault zone. There is no clear evidence of any Holocene activity along this part of the fault. We conclude that the activity of this northerly segment of the Calico Fault is sharply waning or has ceased entirely and that the northern limit of faulting may have retreated southward with time (Miller and others, 2007).

The more southerly part of the Calico Fault near the Lava Bed Mountains and Silver Bell Mine branches into two main strands and several subordinate splays. The primary strands are the Calico Fault and the West Calico Fault. The Calico Fault in this area generally appears to cut deposits no younger than middle to late Pleistocene (Qiao). Although it locally appears to offset Holocene stream channels, these apparent offsets may be inherited from Pleistocene faulting. The West Calico Fault appears to cut middle to late Pleistocene deposits (Qia) southwest of the Silver Bell Mine. , The primary splays of the Calico Fault seem to converge to the southeast along the southwest side of the Lava Bed Mountains.

Rodman Fault

The Rodman Fault was mapped by Bassett and Kupfer (1964) and Dibblee (1964a, 1966), although neither named the fault; the first use of the name Rodman Fault appears to be by Dokka (1983). The Rodman Fault follows the trend of the Bullion Fault, beginning at the northwest corner of the Bullion Mountains and stepping slightly left, terminating at the east edge of the Lava Bed Mountains. Sediments of late Tertiary to early Quaternary age are elevated and highly dissected just south of, and leading up to, the gap between the northern Bullion Fault and the Rodman Fault, suggesting the compressive regime of a left step in a dextral fault system. The Bullion Fault and the Rodman Fault may therefore be linked. The mapped trace of the Rodman Fault is based on fault scarps seen on areal photography. In the Lava Bed Mountains, scarps appear to cut units as young as Qyao, suggesting that the fault may have ruptured in the Holocene.

Galway Lake Fault

The Galway Lake Fault occurs at the south edge of the map area, north of the Emerson Fault and south of the West Calico Fault. Often identified as the Emerson Fault, but locally called the Galway Lake Fault, it has ruptured twice in the last 35 years; it ruptured in the 1975 M_w 5.2 Galway Lake earthquake, showing a right-lateral sense of displacement (Hill and Beeby, 1977) and again in the 1992 M_w 7.5 Landers earthquake. In the Galway Lake earthquake, the fault ruptured along a trace measuring about 6.8 km, although the visible trace is now much shorter. Hill and Beeby (1977) report evidence of earlier slip events on this fault based on geomorphic and trenching evidence. The fault exhibited 9 cm of displacement after the Landers earthquake, although this may have been induced by triggered slip (Hart and others, 1993).

Emerson Fault

The Emerson Fault strikes northwest for ~60 km, extending from Sand Hill, at the south border of the 29 Palms Marine Corps Air-Ground Combat Center, to the north end of the Fry Mountains, where it merges with the Camp Rock Fault (USGS and CGS, 2007); approximately the north half of the fault lies within the Newberry Springs quadrangle. The trace of the mapped fault is based on field observations, aerial photography, and the generalized surface rupture of the 1992 Landers earthquake (USGS and CGS, 2007).

The complex surface rupture of the Landers earthquake spanned nearly the entire north half of the Emerson Fault, including most segments in the Newberry Springs quadrangle, and ended just southeast of the Homestead Valley Fault at the south edge of the map area. Near the junction of the Emerson Fault and the Homestead Valley Fault, the Emerson Fault ruptured across a playa. Trench studies across the ruptures in the playa revealed that one major prehistoric earthquake occurred on the Emerson Fault in the Holocene, approximately 9 ka, and this earthquake was at least locally similar in magnitude to the Landers earthquake (Rubin and Sieh, 1997). The maximum right-lateral displacement recorded for the Landers earthquake occurred on the Emerson Fault, where it crosses Galway Lake Road, west of Galway Lake (Irvine and Hill, 1993). Detailed mapping in this area near Galway Lake Road showed complex patterns of vertical and lateral slip on numerous splays that may represent the initiation of slip transfer to the nearby south end of the Camp Rock Fault (McGill and Rubin, 1999). Primary displacement during the Landers earthquake shifted to the Camp Rock Fault just north of the Bessemer Mine Road. Although mapping immediately following the Landers earthquake indicated that surface rupture on the Emerson Fault continued northward past this junction (USGS and CGS, 2007), there is presently no field evidence for rupture along this strand. This suggests that surface breaks in Holocene deposits can be rapidly erased by subsequent erosion and deposition. We did map traces of the Landers rupture where it cut Pleistocene deposits. Near the Copper Strand Mine, slip from the Landers earthquake is manifested on the Emerson Fault. This zone of surface deformation is only ~300 m long. Traces of the Emerson Fault that did not rupture in the Landers event continue ~2 km northwestward, where they presumably merge with the Camp Rock Fault in the vicinity of the Camp Rock Mine.

Homestead Valley Fault

The Homestead Valley Fault extends only a short distance northwest from the south edge of the map area before merging with the Emerson Fault. While almost the entire length of the Homestead Valley Fault ruptured in the 1992 Landers earthquake, only the northernmost 2 km of the fault is present in the Newberry Springs quadrangle. Hart and others (1993) showed that the Homestead Valley Fault merges complexly with the Emerson Fault.

Camp Rock Fault

The Camp Rock Fault lies between Daggett Ridge and the Newberry Mountains in the north and terminates southward near Iron Ridge. Surface rupture along the Camp Rock Fault during the 1992 Landers earthquake extended northward nearly continuously from Iron Ridge to the west tip of the Rodman Mountains. The mapped trace in the Newberry Springs quadrangle is based on field observations and areal photography and is generalized from the surface-rupture map of the Landers earthquake (USGS and CGS, 2007). Hawkins (1976) estimated >2.0 km offset and Cox and others (1987) estimated 4.1 km of dextral offset on the fault; the latter figure was subsequently corroborated by Jachens and others (2002) on the basis of geophysical data. The fault, as mapped by Dibblee (1970), terminates near the east end of Daggett Ridge. Previous workers have depicted the fault terminating in a number of ways, for example by curving westward and dying out as an oblique reverse fault (Dokka and Travis, 1990) and by dying out within overturned Miocene gravel (Dibblee, 1970). Detailed mapping by Hawkins (1976) supplemented by unpublished mapping by B.F. Cox (personal commun., 2006) demonstrated that three fault strands are present near the apparent termination and that two of the strands actually pass through the hill rather than dying out within it. One of these strands cuts early Holocene alluvial deposits. Cox and Wilshire (1993) mapped the Camp Rock Fault northwest of this area and nearly directly along strike. Their mapping of the Camp Rock Fault lies within a ridge of gravels (QToa) within the piedmont north of Daggett Ridge and passes across the Mojave River to merge with the Harper Lake Fault along the southwest front of the Mitchell Range. The fault zone south of the river has multiple splays as mapped by Cox and Wilshire (1993), but in our reconnaissance we could only find one splay that is mappable at the 1:100,000 scale. Densmore and others (1997) demonstrated that a northwest-striking strand near the south edge of the Mojave River had repeated displacements during the middle and late Holocene. We portray this fault as connecting southward with the Camp Rock Fault by a questionable trace that we could not document with field studies. The main argument for this questionable trace is based on the nearly perfect alignment of recently active fault strands on opposite sides of the piedmont and the lack of fault rupture or geomorphic evidence for other geometries. However, the strands are separated by a 6-km-long gap where the piedmont alluvial fans show no clear evidence of faulting.

Johnson Valley Fault

The Johnson Valley Fault begins south of the map area and enters the map area in the Fry Mountains. We mapped the fault approximately 2.5 km further north than it had been previously mapped. In this zone, the fault clearly cuts late Pleistocene (Qia) deposits and may offset Holocene deposits. South of the map area, Rockwell and others (2000) determined that the segment of the Johnson Valley Fault at Melville dry lake last ruptured ~5.8 ka and had at least two older Holocene ruptures. Further north, the fault bends to the northwest and crosses the northwestern Fry Mountains. There is no evidence that the fault cuts Quaternary deposits in the valley southeast of the East Ord Mountains. However, we tentatively recognize a northeast-striking fault along the southeastern front of the East Ord Mountains, and this feature may be a northward extension of the Johnson Valley Fault. If so, then it may merge to the north with the Camp Rock Fault.

Dolores Lake Fault

Dibblee and Bassett (1966a) and Meek (1994) described the Dolores Lake Fault extending north-northwest from the west side of Harvard Hill to Coyote Lake, on the basis of scarps and anomalous topography. North of the Newberry Springs quadrangle, the fault cuts Pleistocene, but not Holocene, deposits (Dudash, 2006). Along its southern extent, however, it is defined by uplifted latest Pleistocene Mojave River gravels (Meek, 1994), which suggests Holocene activity. The Manix and Dolores Lake Faults intersect southwest of Harvard Hill, where Lake Manix deposits are uplifted along the fault. These relations suggest that late Pleistocene deformation is pronounced and is possibly attributable to local compression between the faults.

Lenwood Fault

The Lenwood Fault, as mapped by Dibblee (1964b, 1970), occurs in the southwestern region of the Newberry Springs quadrangle. It crosses the western part of Daggett Ridge, where a complex network of fault splays is well exposed. Several strands of the Lenwood Fault are present, with one or more cutting middle Holocene deposits (Qyay). At a prominent right step in the fault at Daggett Ridge, a small playa occupies a graben, where vertical offsets create easily identifiable fault scarps. The primary evidence for youthful movements along the Lenwood Fault includes scarps in Holocene alluvial fan deposits and the elongate, straight-sided hills of unconsolidated gravel (QToa) in Stoddard Valley. There, the steep, straight margins of these hills are aligned with straight washes and canyons farther east, all anomalously trending across prevailing topographic gradients. Another possible fault adjacent to the Lenwood Fault lies farther north and east of the Lenwood Fault, splaying off and striking nearly due north in eastern Stoddard Valley. This fault loses expression farther north, as if dying out.

In the southern part of the map area, the Lenwood Fault cuts middle to late Pleistocene deposits (Qia) at various places between the south edge of the map area and Tyler Valley near the center of the Ord Mountains. Paleoseismology at Soggy Lake, south of the map area, shows that surface ruptures formed along the southern Lenwood Fault at 1.8±0.2 ka and 8.2±0.2 ka (Padgett and Rockwell, 1994). To the north in Tyler Valley, the fault cuts alluvial deposits of latest Pleistocene to early Holocene age (Qyao).

Tin Can Alley Fault

The Tin Can Alley Fault, named and mapped north of the map area by Dudash (2006), is difficult to identify where it enters the Newberry Springs quadrangle at the east edge of the Calico Mountains. Several Pleistocene alluvial deposits appear to be warped, uplifted, and stranded and to possibly contain eroded fault scarps in the zone where we map the fault and nearby splays, but it is difficult to find a single unambiguous fault scarp. A shallow pediment developed on Miocene strata creates some of the ambiguities. Dudash did not observe the Tin Can Alley Fault cutting Holocene deposits and, therefore, considered the latest displacements to be Pleistocene in age.

Harper Lake Fault

Along the Mitchell Range, the Harper Lake Fault is roughly colinear with the Camp Rock Fault but does not cut any young deposits. The youngest deposit within which we found scarps or other evidence of faulting is an early late Pleistocene alluvial fan deposit (Qiao). The fault apparently has a large up-to-the-northeast component of offset, judging from topography. We are puzzled by the relatively early age of latest fault rupture that we determined for the Harper Lake Fault, as opposed to the middle to late Holocene ages that Densmore and others (1997) determined for the nearby fault strands south of the Mojave River. Further studies, including detailed mapping and possibly trenching, are needed to reconcile these apparent differences.

The Fault Database

Faults are mapped as linear features in the database, with associated information attached to the line or series of lines that make up a particular fault. Fault segments on the major faults are named; fault segments not belonging to major faults are unnamed. The name of the fault, or the designation "unnamed", are recorded in the accompanying database. Four types of information are associated with faults: name, uncertainty category, exposure, and notes on the geomorphic evidence that supports the mapping of the fault.

Information regarding faulting uncertainty is divided into three categories that rate the likelihood that a fault exists:

Certain—Reserved for faults that can be traced unambiguously. These faults are mapped by geomorphic features traceable by stereo-pair areal photographs or other remote-sensing techniques and have at least one fault exposure, either observed in outcrop or in a trench. The requirement of an observed exposure in outcrop is relaxed for faults mapped as "certain" in previous geologic map publications, provided the geomorphic evidence is strong

Probable—Faults lacking an observed exposure but having multiple lines of indirect evidence supporting their existence, for example lineaments, topographic scarps, offset streams, shutter ridges, pop ups, sag ponds or depressions, and lithologic contrasts

Possible—Faults with one or two indirect-evidence features, possibly also clues such as an orientation consistent with the grain of more certain faults in the area

We map Quaternary faulting only and do not attempt to display older faults. However, where the age of the fault is ambiguous, we include faults that might be Quaternary in age.

Whether or not a fault cuts the unit it traverses or is concealed beneath the unit is recorded in the database.

Exposed—Faults cut the unit or units they traverse, and are therefore inferred to be younger than the units they cut

Concealed—Faults that are inferred to be concealed beneath, and older than, units they traverse. In some instances concealed faults separate two different types of units in the database. In this case there is a contact separating the units, but it is spatially coincident with the concealed fault in map view and is therefore not included as a separate line object in the database.

The database field contains brief notes on the types of geomorphic features observed, as follows:

Geomorphic scarps—Scarps and steps in piedmonts, steep hillslopes, hillslope lineaments, exposed hillslope material (commonly high-albedo calcium carbonate layers)

Offset streams—Streams that show apparent lateral offset

Steepened streams—Streams that show abrupt changes in gradient

Lithologic contrast—Contrasting lithology suggestive of fault contact, usually aligned in many exposures that together suggest that a fault is the cause of the lithologic contrast.

The symbolization of exposed faults departs from standard geologic map symbology. Exposed faults are symbolized by the degree of uncertainty of existence, rather than uncertainty in location (faults that are concealed by alluvial material are symbolized according to the conventional symbolization for concealed faults). We feel that the uncertainty of the existence of faults is more important to the interpretation of the tectonic and derivative fault studies than the locational uncertainty of a given fault. Traditional geologic mapping does not distinguish clearly between the types of uncertainty (age, location, existence), nor does it offer clear symbolization differences that separate these qualities. Whether or not a fault exists, that is, whether or not the geology has been properly mapped and interpreted, is critical not only to tectonic interpretation but also to land-use planning and to addressing regulatory issues.

The locational uncertainty is included in the database, but at the 1:100,000 scale it probably is not particularly meaningful. We use this as an example of the power and value of the database—to modify the map symbolization to best communicate the geologic relations central to our mapping.

Quaternary Volcanic Rocks

The map area contains several Quaternary volcanic centers and flows, including volcanic rocks associated with the Pisgah and Sunshine Peak cones.

The Pisgah cone and associated lava flows were mapped in detail by Wise (1966) and in reconnaissance by Dibblee (1966). Wise (1966) distinguished three distinct flows for Pisgah crater and two flows for Sunshine crater using basalt rheology. He separated the Sunshine crater basalts into the Lavic Flow and the Sunshine Flow. Both Wise and Dibblee suspected the lavas were Quaternary in age, but recently analytical ages were obtained from the lavas. M. Lanphere obtained an $^{40}Ar/^{39}Ar$ plateau age of 18.3±2.6 ka and an isochron age of 23.4±4.3 ka (Sylvester and others, 2002) for the second of the three eruptive phases that flowed from the Pisgah Cone. Phillips (2003) obtained a mean age of 22.5±1.3 ka using cosmogenic ^{26}Cl, sampling within the first (oldest) Pisgah Flow. This age assumes an erosion rate of 1 *mm/yr*. Other dates obtained by Phillips (2003) vary from an oldest date of 24.2±2.7 (assuming an erosion rate of 0 *mm/yr*) to 18.9±1.6 Ka (assuming a 5 *mm/yr* erosion rate). Age estimates based on calibrated desert varnish microstratigraphy yield a similar age range of 24 to 30 ka (Liu, 2003). The various dating methods yield similar ages and place the age of the oldest Pisgah flow at very late Pleistocene. Furthermore, Champion (personal commun., 2007) suggests that all three of the Pisgah Flows erupted within a short time frame (<20 years) on the basis of the similarity of paleomagnetic orientations within the flows.

The Sunshine Peak flow has not been dated, nor has paleomagnetic data been recorded for the flow.

A lava field, referred to as the Pipkin Lava Field by Oskin and others (2007), occupies a paleovalley floor and is perched southeast of Newberry Springs in the Newberry Mountains. The valley has been truncated on the north side by a steep escarpment sloping down to the Troy Lake area. Oskin and others (2007) acquired an average $^{40}Ar/^{39}Ar$ age of 770±40 ka.

Broadwell Lake

Broadwell Lake is an active playa in an enclosed topographic basin north of the town of Ludlow. It has an elongate shape, roughly 7 km long and 2 km wide at its broadest point, oriented north-south, and covers an area of roughly 8.5 km^2. It receives runoff from the eastern Cady Mountains, western Bristol Mountains, and mountains south of the town of Ludlow.

Broadwell Lake is distinguished by long, linear fissures that cross the playa trending approximately 40°. More than 50 linear fissures over 60 m long appear on maps created by EMCON Associates (1993), Rasmussen and Associates (1990), and Dibblee (1967b). In addition, there are polygonal fissures at the broad, north end of the playa.

Fissures on playas in general have been extensively studied by Neil (1968) and Neil and others (1968), and the fissures of Broadwell Lake in particular have been investigated by EMCON Associates (1993) and Rasmussen and Associates (1990) as part of a feasibility study for siting a low-level nuclear waste storage facility. Curiously, Broadwell Lake appears in the study by Neal and others (1968) as a playa without fissures, although it is unlikely that the fissures on Broadwell Lake are less than 40 years old.

Neal and others (1968) described giant desiccation polygons on 39 playas across the southwestern United States. They classified them into two general types: polygonal desiccation features and linear desiccation features. Polygonal desiccation features, called giant desiccation polygons, are formed when fissures intersect at angles, forming polygons, and can be from 15 to 300 m across. Fresh cracks quickly become wedge shaped as the sides cave in and they fill with sediment. Older desiccation features commonly consist of vegetated linear mounds. They presumably initially acquire vegetation where water and sediments pond along the fissures, then gradually expand into coppice mounds as vegetation traps more sediment, and finally coalesce into linear accretionary mounds. Messina and others (2005) proposed a life cycle for desiccation features: a new fissure forms in the subsurface and propagates vertically in both directions until it creates a surface rupture. It then begins to fill with sediment and eventually acquires vegetation and forms constructional mounds along the former site of the fissure. In time, the mounds are eroded to the playa base level, until all that remains on the playa surface is a slight discoloration that contrasts with the surrounding sediment.

Linear desiccation features, called giant desiccation stripes by Neal and others (1968), are presumably formed in a manner similar to giant desiccation polygons, but the linear features do not intersect at angles; rather, they form roughly perpendicular to the playa shoreline. They have only been observed on long, narrow playas, and have not been seen as fresh cracks. Existing giant desiccation stripes are only observed as constructional, vegetated features (Neal and others, 1968).

Broadwell Lake contains both types of giant desiccation features; the giant desiccation stripes are by far the most abundant and the most prominent. The giant desiccation polygons are marked by dark staining, minor depressions, and occasional sinks, and the giant desiccation stripes are long, parallel, constructional ridges of fine materials approximately 0.5 to 1 m high that are vegetated and trend approximately 45° NE. The stripes, designated type 1 features by EMCON Associates (1993), were trenched in four places by Rasmussen and Associates (1990) and found to extend to approximately 3 m in depth. Viewed in cross section, the stripes are wedge-shaped fissures that are wider at the top due to the collapse of the edges subsequent to the fissures formation. Rasmussen and Associates (1990) report a sandy marker bed, approximately 12 cm thick, near the bottom of all four trenches. The marker bed is not offset in any of the trenches, which indicates that the fissures are not faulted vertically. Moreover, the intact nature of the marker bed indicates that the fissures are not faults, which would disrupt the uncemented playa sediments even after strike-slip fault movement. The ends of the larger fissures extend beyond the bounds of the modern playa and into the playa fringe deposits on the east side of Broadwell Lake. The playa fringe deposits are decadal or centennial in age. It is likely that the fissures pre-date the playa fringe, because the roughness of the vegetated and cobbly playa fringe deposits would have inhibited the formation of the constructional ridges. This suggests that the fissures probably existed well into the past, when the Broadwell Lake shoreline extended higher up the alluvial fan.

The giant desiccation stripes on Broadwell Lake have one property that separates them from giant desiccation stripes observed on other playas: they are not parallel to the playa shoreline. In fact, their trend is remarkably uniform (approximately 45° NE.) through the entire length of the playa and apparently independent of the direction of the shoreline. This suggests that the giant desiccation stripes either formed perpendicular to some older playa shoreline that pre-dates the current shoreline or that they formed in response to a stress field unrelated to any that might have been created by the edges of the playa. The latter implies that a relatively uniform extensional stress oriented roughly 45° NW. (perpendicular to the direction of fissure propagation) existed at some point in the recent past and that the fissures formed in response to the stress.

Mojave River Plain

The Mojave River traverses the northern part of the Newberry Springs quadrangle. It lies within a narrow valley about 12 km long between Barstow and Daggett, where a variety of Miocene and younger strata flank the valley, and alluvial fans shed from Daggett Ridge locally extend to the river. At Daggett and extending east for more than 30 km, the river enters an unconfined reach over which it spread widely in the past to form a broad plain (fig. 2). The river currently is incised into this broad plain by 4 to 8 m and is bordered by inset terraces that are interpreted to be middle Holocene in age (QywyMR) on the basis of geomorphology and soils. This is consistent with Pleistocene ^{14}C ages of deposits shallowly buried in the plain (Reynolds and Reynolds, 1985). The plain extends east beyond Newberry Springs on the south to Manix Wash on the north and extends farther north to Coyote Lake in the adjacent Soda Mountains quadrangle, an area of approximately 400 km[2]. Over much of this plain, relic channel patterns are evident as subtle ridge crests that branch in the downstream direction. The surficial deposits underlying the channel patterns consist of sandy grus gravels with distinctive reddish quartzite clasts indicative of Mojave River deposits; other deposits of the plain are finer grained and mostly sand and mud. We consider the channel forms to represent inverted stream-channel deposits. The channels are oriented nearly northward in the area north of Daggett and west of Yermo and also in the area between Harvard Hill and Coyote Lake (Hagar, 1966; Groat, 1967; Meek, 1990). Elsewhere they mainly branch eastward, forming fan-like patterns that mimic the geometry of the plain. The mean grain size of deposits of the plain and the degree to which inverted channels stand out from the plain both decrease eastward. As a result, near Troy Lake and near Manix Wash (fig. 2), deposits are primarily sand size and the surface has minimal relief.

The plain has been modified by deposition of eolian sand derived from the Mojave River, which defines a sand-transport path leading east to the Cady Mountains. The plain is also deeply incised near Manix Wash, where Jefferson (2003) and previous workers have defined underlying Pleistocene strata of Lake Manix. At several locations along the Manix Fault system, tectonic pop-ups have deformed the plain. At these sites, older Mojave River deposits and lake deposits, with well developed soils, attest to shortening where faults intersect. Prime examples are at the intersections with the Calico and Dolores Lake Faults (fig. 3). The Calico Fault creates a down-to-the-northeast step in the plain that is 1 to 3 m in height, and complex in detail. Although poorly exposed, the pale color of deposits west of the fault may indicate past groundwater-discharge.

The plain possesses soils that mark it as roughly equivalent in age to alluvial deposit Qyao, which is dated in many places in the eastern Mojave Desert as about 9 to 15 ka (Mahan and others, 2007). Locally, Reynolds and Reynolds (1985) dated a section that they interpreted as representing ponds within the fluvial plain at 12.8±0.9 to 9.05±0.35 ^{14}C ka (uncalibrated). Strata of the plain apparently overlie the uppermost lacustrine or deltaic unit of Jefferson (2003) at Manix Wash, which he considers to be about [14]C 19 ka (uncalibrated).

Late Pliocene–Late Pleistocene Playa and Lake Deposits along the Mojave River Valley (Manix formation and Mojave River formation)

The north-central part of the Newberry Springs quadrangle includes bedded and laminated, fine- to coarse-grained, conglomeratic late Pliocene to late Pleistocene deposits that provide a relatively complete record of playa, lake, and alluvial environments that preceded establishment of the through-going, eastward-flowing Mojave River. During the latter part of this time period (middle to late Pleistocene), Lake Manix was an ephemeral pluvial lake (fig. 6) and it probably was the largest in a chain of lakes that extended along the current Mojave River drainage (Jefferson and Reynolds, 1985; Enzel and others, 2003; Jefferson, 2003). At its high stand of 543 m above mean sea level, it formed a tri-lobed lake with one lobe occupying the Afton Basin, which extended east from the Manix Wash area to about the Afton Canyon area in the adjacent Soda Mountains quadrangle. The map area includes the western part of the Afton Basin and the Troy Lake Basin of ancient Lake Manix; whereas, the adjacent Soda Mountains quadrangle contains the eastern part of the Afton and Coyote Lake Basins or lobes (fig. 6). In latest Pleistocene time (after about 18 ka), incision of Afton Canyon, east of the map area in the Soda Mountains quadrangle, drained much of Lake Manix and initiated the current, through-going eastward drainage of this basin by the Mojave River (Meek, 1999; Enzel and others, 2003; Jefferson, 2003). Further downcutting by the Mojave River eventually exposed middle to late Pleistocene beds of Lake Manix, as well as the underlying late Pliocene to early Pleistocene playa and alluvial deposits (Mojave River formation) that pre-date Lake Manix.

In keeping with our scheme for surficial geologic mapping of Quaternary and late Tertiary sediments, we mapped and assigned unit labels to these late Pliocene-early Pleistocene sediments based on their ages and deposit type (QTop, Qoa, Qil, Qilf, Qilc, Qilg). The resulting units shown on this map and their relations and correlations with previously mapped and described units of the Mojave River formation of Nagy and Murray (1991) and the Manix formation of Jefferson (2003) are included in the discussion below.

The older and lower part of this late Pliocene to early Pleistocene sequence of closed-basin sediments was first studied and described in detail by Nagy and Murray (1991). They described a >80-m-thick, partly gypsiferous, sequence of reddish-brown and buff clay, silt, and sand beds, and they presented data from geochemical correlation of ash interbeds and paleomagnetic data that suggest the sequence ranges in age from about 2.6 to 0.8 Ma and may have a preferred age range of about 2.1 to 1.1 Ma (see also, Pluhar and others, 1991; Nagy and Murray, 1996). Nagy and Murray (1991) also informally named this late Pliocene to early Pleistocene, coarsening-upward sequence the Mojave River formation, and they discussed sedimentological characteristics of these beds that suggest they were deposited in playa or saline lake and alluvial environments. Their investigations focused on prominent exposures east of Manix Wash along the south side of Buwalda Ridge, where these beds are tilted and folded along the Manix Fault, and on exposures south of Buwalda Ridge and the Mojave River; they also noted that the Mojave River formation extends farther east, perhaps as far as Afton Canyon. Our mapping of these deposits (QTop) agrees with that assertion and we have traced these playa-lacustrine and alluvial deposits of the Mojave River formation farther eastward than Manix Wash and northward and northeastward into the adjacent Soda Mountains quadrangle.

Near Manix Wash, Buwalda Ridge, and farther northeast in the adjacent Soda Mountains quadrangle, Lake Manix beds commonly overlie the Mojave River formation. Buwalda (1914) first reported on the Lake Manix beds near Buwalda Ridge. Jefferson and Reynolds (1985) later described these lake deposits in detail, based on exposures along Manix Wash and near Buwalda Ridge, and he informally named them the Manix formation. Jefferson and Reynolds (1985) informally divide the Manix formation into four ascending members (A, B, C, and D). McGill and others (1988) mapped these units in detail along Manix Wash, north of the Mojave River. As discussed by Jefferson and Reynolds (1985) and Jefferson (2003) and as mapped by McGill and others (1988), these informal members of the Manix formation locally intertongue and the lower members (A and B) show both concordant and discordant contacts and perhaps even gradational contacts (see below) with the underlying beds of the Mojave River formation (QTop).

Member A of the Manix formation (Jefferson and Reynolds, 1985; Jefferson, 2003) is a cobble to boulder fanglomerate that occurs along the north flank of the Cady Mountains and is mostly confined to the south side of the Mojave River; it is not exposed, or does not occur, in the area mapped by McGill and others (1988) along Manix Wash and Buwalda Ridge on the north side of the Mojave River. South of Manix Wash and Buwalda Ridge on the south side of the Mojave River, however, member A overlies the Mojave River formation, and Nagy and Murray (1991, 1996) reported that relations observed there suggest that this fanglomerate (Jefferson's member A) is in transitional contact with the underlying Mojave River formation. They also discuss paleomagnetic data (Pluhar and others, 1991) from which an age in the range of about 0.78 to 1.1

20

Ma can be inferred for the basal part of member A. Meek and Battles (1991) note that this fanglomerate, at least in part, records Pleistocene uplift of the Cady Mountains along the south side of the Mojave River. Because the unit is principally a coarse fanglomerate that contains stage III and stage IV pedogenic carbonate, we mapped it as an older Quaternary fan deposit (Qoa); this assignment attaches a middle to early Pleistocene age to these deposits that is in agreement with previous age estimates (for example Nagy and Murray, 1991, 1996; Jefferson, 2003).

Members B, C, and D of the Manix formation (Jefferson and Reynolds, 1985; Jefferson, 2003) are primarily confined to exposures along the north side of the Mojave River. Of these three members, member C, which consists mainly of bedded to laminated green clay to sandy silt beds, is the most distinctive and was interpreted by Jefferson as a deep lake deposit. Members B and D are principally whitish to buff, sandy, and locally pebbly and cobbly beds that principally underlie and overlie, respectively, the fine-grained green beds of member C. Members B and D, and particularly member B, also interfinger with member C. As noted by McGill and others (1988) and also as mapped locally by Jefferson, member B has both concordant and discordant contacts with the underlying Mojave River formation. Member B may include both subaerial and subaqueous deposits and probably in part represents sandy, distal alluvial fan deposits shed southward from the Alvord Mountains (Jefferson and Reynolds, 1985; McGill and others, 1988). The uppermost member (member D) apparently represents alluvial plain and delta sediments deposited along the western margin of Lake Manix during latest Pleistocene time as the Mojave River's clastic wedge prograded into the lake basin. Jefferson and Reynolds (1985) and Jefferson (2003) present and discuss paleontological evidence and other age data, which collectively imply that the combined age range of members B and C extends from about >350 ka (perhaps as much as 500) to about 60 ka, and imply that member D ranges in age from about 60 to 19 ka. For our surficial geologic mapping, we mapped and partly subdivided these lacustrine and lake-margin deposits as follows: Qil, lake sediments, undivided; Qilf, fine-grained lake sediment (principally Jefferson's member C); Qilc, coarse-grained lake and alluvial sediments (Jefferson's members B or D); Qilg, lacustrine beach gravels.

Groundwater Discharge Deposits

Ground-water discharge deposits were highlighted by Forester and others (2002) as an important class of desert deposits formed in spring and wetland settings that are commonly misinterpreted as lake or playa deposits. Following studies by Quade and others (1995, 2003), Forester and others described the deposits in hydrologic terms: springs are point discharge sites and wetlands result from dispersed discharge. Both create characteristic calcium-carbonate rich deposits with common charophyte, ostracode and diatom fossils and less common gastropods, plant impressions, and peat (black mat). Low-discharge springs commonly form convex upward mound-like deposits, whereas wetlands form deposits with gentle dips, commonly as perched benches in distal alluvial piedmont positions. Sediments in both are off-white to pale green and pale brown, and predominantly fine sands and silts.

Pedogenesis

We separate Quaternary deposits in the Mojave Desert into four age groups using an idealized soil chronosequence (described below and referenced in the following paragraphs), which we refer to as active, young, intermediate, and old. Soil chronosequences, originally defined by Jenny (1941), offer a way to estimate the age of a geologic unit based on its soil characteristics, assuming that parent material, topography, climate, and organic processes remain relatively constant. The idealized chronosequence that we use is based on the following concepts of soil formation. Soils in the Mojave Desert develop by acquiring wind-born silt and clay, which infiltrates into the soil and forms a succession of soil horizons. Initially the silt accumulates to form an A_v horizon. Through time a textural B horizon is formed, and carbonate accumulates in the soil, eventually concentrating in a carbonate K horizon. Clays and carbonate can accumulate in the B horizon, forming a B_t or B_{tk} horizon, and oxidation typically turns the horizon a deep red to reddish-brown color. The concentration of carbonate in the K horizon in coarse-grained soils begins by first coating large clasts underneath, then completely coating the clasts as the carbonate rind thickens, then filling voids and bridging the clasts, forming laminations within the carbonate material, and finally producing a brecciated texture and large pisoliths. Using this idealized model for soil development, approximate ages can be assigned to soils based on their degree of soil development. This pedogenic progression is modified by local circumstances (for example, availability of carbonate in the parent material, climate factors, vegetation, and availability of eolian fines from nearby sources). When the effect of elevation on climate is considered, we generally assume that the rate of soil development is the same across the mapped area and that soils having roughly the same morphology are therefore roughly the same age. Fig. 7 shows the conceptual model of soil development used for mapping geomorphic surfaces in the map area.

The idealized chronosequence model that we use is based on a large body of work spanning 40 years of studying soil development in desert environments, primarily the southwestern United States, including New Mexico and the Mojave Desert. Gile (1966) described four morphological stages of carbonate accumulation in soils: bottoms of pebbles coated, bottoms and tops coated, interstices cemented, and laminar texture forming in the carbonate. He places an age of middle to late Holocene on the first stage and early to middle Holocene on the second stage and states that the entire sequence can be completed since late Pleistocene. Machette (1985) described two additional stages of carbonate development, where carbonate forms pisoliths and where multiple episodes of pisolith formation and brecciation are evident. The carbonate is derived primarily from eolian dust and, therefore, accumulates in soils regardless of parent lithology, although parent lithology can enhance carbonate accumulation, especially around surface clasts (McFadden and others, 1998). Eolian dust accumulation in soils within the Mojave Desert seems to have been greatest in the early Holocene and is attributed to a drying of the climate, which created ephemeral lakes (playas) as significant sources of dust input (Wells and others, 1987; Reheis and others, 1995). Recent studies (Reheis and others, 1995; Reynolds and others, 2006) have determined that the A_v horizon in early Holocene soils at numerous sites in southern California and southern Nevada is similar in composition to modern eolian dust, implicating dust as the probable source for much of the A_v horizon. Eolian dust also affects surface morphology by helping to create desert pavements. McFadden and others (1983, 1984) noted the increase of eolian fines with increasing age on isolated volcanic surfaces of the Cima volcanic field that could not receive water-deposited sediment. They noted the presence of an A_v horizon on the youngest desert pavement surfaces and that, with increasing age of the volcanic flow, the A_v horizon below the stone pavement thickened and the soil developed into a B_w then B_t horizon. The interiors of peds from the A_v horizon are more reddened and have a higher carbonate concentration than the faces and, with depth, the soils transition from A_v to AB to B, indicating that the A_v horizon thickens with time and develops into the B horizon. Further work by Wells and others (1995) established that the stones that make up the desert pavement remain at the land surface throughout the soil development history. The soils, therefore, are accretionary, and the A_v horizons continue to accumulate beneath the stone pavements, lifting the stones higher as the soil profile grows. Older soils buried by younger soils provide evidence that significant A_v development may occur in pulses (McFadden and others, 1983), and thermo-luminescence dates from A_v horizons in the Cima volcanic field indicate that

22

the horizons have a mean age of middle Holocene, which is ascribed to the mixing of young and old A_v material (McFadden and others, 1998). Reheis and others (1989), working near Silver Lake playa, placed an age range of 1—8 ka on geomorphic surfaces with soil development similar to soils classified as Quaternary young alluvial deposits for this report. Recent optically stimulated luminescence dates indicate ages of 4–7 ka for younger surfaces in this group and 11–17 ka for older surfaces (Sohn and others, 2007), implying that the age of Quaternary young surfaces is generally latest Pleistocene to middle Holocene. This is in agreement with Mahan and others (2007), who date younger surfaces in this group as approximately 3 to 5 ka and an older surface in this group as approximately 12 ka. Sohn and others (2007) also date deposits with well-developed desert pavements (intermediate fan units in this report) as approximately 25 ka, and Mahan and others (2007) provide an age range of 33 to 140 ka, which is consistent with an approximate age of late Pleistocene. The general model of soil development and age (fig. 7) was developed from these and similar investigations.

Desert Pavements

Desert pavements are unique and interesting features in many deserts throughout the world that form when eolian fines, primarily silt, are trapped and accumulate beneath the surface, lifting and concentrating larger clasts at the surface (McFadden and others, 1983; Wells and others, 1995; Anderson, 1999). However, many of the specific processes are not well understood. We include some general observations regarding desert pavements in the Newberry Springs quadrangle to contribute to further research into their formation and development through time.

Throughout the manuscript, we refer to pavement as weakly, moderately, or strongly developed desert pavement. These modifiers refer to the overall development of a desert pavement, which includes a number of factors: the darkness of varnish, the degree that surface stones (primarily pebbles and cobbles) interlock, the degree of rubification (weak to strong) on the undersides of the surface stones, the degree to which surface stones are embedded in the A_v horizon immediately beneath them, and the degree of flatness of the surface (devoid of bar-and-swale topography). If a pavement exhibits all or many of these properties, it is described as strongly developed; if it exhibits only one or two of these properties, it is classified as weakly developed.

A typical desert pavement consists of moderately to strongly varnished, interlocking stones over a silty to fine-sandy A_v horizon (fig. 8). The bottoms of the surface stones are often embedded in the A_v horizon immediately beneath them, so that light force is required to dislodge them. The undersides are moderately to strongly rubified. However, desert pavements are variable in structure; they can have interlocking stones that have slightly dark varnish (fig. 9), or have darkly varnished stones that do not interlock but have an exposed A_v or B_t horizon in the interstices. The former are interpreted as young pavements, the latter as older degrading pavements, if all clasts are composed of lithologies capable of acquiring varnish. In environments where eolian sand is deposited, desert pavements have fewer armor stones, tend to be noninterlocking, and have an abundance of sand in the interstices at the surface and in the A_v horizon (fig. 10). Mafic source rocks tend to varnish easily and quite darkly, while felsic rocks can exhibit little or no varnish. The degree of varnish on desert pavements depends significantly on lithology, among other factors.

Ages of deposits capped by desert pavements vary from early Holocene to late middle Pleistocene. Mahan (2007) estimated ages of several alluvial units using luminescence methods. A deposit with weakly developed desert pavement (Qyao) near Baker, California, was found to be approximately 12 ka, and deposits with strongly developed desert pavements (Qiay), near Fort Irwin near Baker, California, were found to be 31–38 ka. Machette (2008) used cosmogenic dating to estimate the ages of deposits associated with several strongly developed desert pavements in Death Valley, California. Unit Qiay was found to be approximately 40–100 ka, and older, more heavily dissected pavements (Qiao), were found to be approximately 130–170 ka. Sohn and others (2007) published slightly younger dates, approximately 25 ka for deposits with well-developed desert pavements. Although the dates, particularly the cosmogenic dates, have a high reported variance, in general it seems that strongly developed desert pavements appear to be no younger than latest Pleistocene, and can be as old as latest middle Pleistocene.

An important land management concern is the stability of pavement surfaces and how fast desert pavements "heal", or re-establish an armored surface, after they have been disturbed. This information can help establish measures of reference-condition behavior, as distinguished from perturbed conditions that may include significant amounts of anthropogenic disturbance. It can also help land managers decide how best to address the human impact on the desert landscape.

Desert pavements can exhibit natural features that indicate how the armor on the surfaces is changing. First, pavement clasts are often darkly varnished on their exposed surfaces and rubified on their underside. Rubification can be used as an indicator of overturned clasts. Since rubification takes place on the underside of pavement clasts, clasts that have rubified sides exposed have been in place long enough for the rubification to occur before being overturned. Such clasts are common on some pavements but quite rare on others. It is not clear whether the clasts are overturned due to erosion or bioturbation. Second, evidence of pavements acquiring new clasts exists in the form of glass and artifact flakes incorporated into the pavement surface. The flakes must relate to Native American activity in the desert, while glass is a modern addition. Figure 11 shows blue glass from a bottle broken on the pavement. Some of the glass shards are now stones in the pavement, underlain by silt and interwoven into the existing pavement clasts. The process that forms the pavement in this area must, therefore, be currently active and able to incorporate stones on a decadal scale. Third, faint transverse bars can often be observed in outcrop perpendicular to flow direction on some pavements (Wells and others, 1985) (fig. 12) and are occasionally visible in high-resolution color imagery, such as aerial photographs from the national agricultural imagery program (NAIP). In general, the bars consist of sand and very fine gravel and are oriented perpendicular to maximum gradient on the pavement, which suggests that running water was involved in their formation. Adjacent swales associated with these bars are made of unvarnished gravel- to sand-sized particles that form a thin veneer on the A_v horizon. The B horizon is not exposed in the swales, which indicates that, although the surface is unarmored in these areas, either the weathering process is too slow to cut into the easily erodable A_v horizon or the swales do not remain exposed for long. The latter implies that an active pavement resurfacing process is underway. These observations indicate that, at least in some areas, desert pavements are active enough to cause visible changes on a decadal timescale.

These time frames for the natural replacement of stones on a pavement surface are supported by previous observations in the literature. Cooke (1970) photographed a roughly 1 m^2 plot of desert pavement one year after it was stripped of its layer of stone armor. The plot shows about 5% recovery of pavement stones, while approximately 1 kg of fine sediment was removed. Engel and Sharp (1958) describe varnished pavement clasts from a road, bladed in 1931 to a level of at least 2 inches deep on the upslope side. The pavement itself is not carefully described, but included diagrams indicate roughly 50% recovery of stone clasts. Sharon (1962) described study plots on hamadas (desert pavement) in Israel 5 years after the removal of 90% of the stone cover. The new hamada consisted primarily of smaller clasts than the surrounding hamada but was 60% to 80% covered in some patches. The pavement recovery was accompanied by a lowering of the fine-sediment surface beneath the stone pavement cover of 15–20 mm, on average.

In conclusion it appears that, in some areas at least, desert pavements can reform armor within decades, but may lose fine material originally beneath the stone pavement before the armor can reform.

Explanation of Map-Unit labels

Map-Unit labels

We separate Quaternary units into four primary age groups, based on the deposit and surface characteristics, the degree of soil development and landforms, and the assumption that similar soils and landforms have similar ages: active (a), young (y), intermediate (i), and old (o). Of these primary groups, the young and intermediate units evolve most rapidly and vary enough to be subdivided into secondary younger (y) and older (o) subclasses.

Active units have received sediment in the past few years or decades. Active alluvial units, for example, have received fluvial sediments deposited in alluvial fan channels and overbank areas in the past few years or decades. Active playas have accumulated fine-grained detrital sediment, and possibly evaporite minerals, as a result of recent flooding, which commonly has alternated with periods of eolian deposition or erosion. Active units, which cover approximately 240 km^2 in the map area, are most likely to affect human activity, since they are geomorphically unstable and susceptible to flooding.

Young units have received sediment in the latest Pleistocene and Holocene but not in the past 100 years or so. Young alluvial units begin to develop when the active sediment supply is cut off by stream capture, diversion, avulsion, or incision. Subsequently, the abandoned surface flattens over time due to diffusive processes such as sheet flow, rain splash, bioturbation, and eolian deposition. Soil development begins with the advent of these diffusive processes, particularly the input of eolian fines (see Pedogenesis). Of the four primary age groups, young units cover the largest part of the map area, more than 2,000 km^2. Other young units within the area include young playas and groundwater-discharge areas. Although not extensive, such units are important for establishing regional stratigraphic correlations. Additionally, active spring deposits and playas are wildlife habitat areas that can play an important role in land management decisions.

Intermediate units are interpreted to be primarily late Pleistocene in age, from ~250 ka to ~10 ka, although the older units may be latest middle Pleistocene, >125 ka. They cover approximately 500 km^2 of the map area. These units have had sufficient time to develop mature soils and desert pavements (see Pedogenesis). They are subdivided on the basis of pedogenic features, such as the thickness of desert varnish and abundance and structure of the soil. Intermediate units are particularly important as recorders of Quaternary fault activity, because they are the youngest units that reliably preserve fault scarps.

Old units are estimated to be early to middle Pleistocene in age, from ~1 Ma to ~250 ka. These units are not aerially extensive and cover only about 60 km^2 in the map area, where only alluvial units were mapped as old. These units typically are higher than younger units, often by several meters, and are usually best preserved adjacent to mountain fronts. Associated landforms tend to be broadly rounded rather than planar, and associated soils typically are severely eroded. The cemented K (carbonate) horizon is commonly at or near the land surface, and the exposure of this highly resistant layer seems to stabilize the surface of the unit, which reduces the rate of subsequent erosion. The age of these units is interpreted to be early to middle Pleistocene.

In addition to age, distinctions of process, environment, and lithology are also made. The major processes and environments ranked by aerial extent are alluvial (a), wash (w), eolian (e), and playa (p). Other processes and environments include mass movement (m) and groundwater-discharge (g). Processes are also subdivided when possible. Alluvial fan deposits formed by debris flows (d), eolian sand ramps (r), sheets (s), and dunes (d) are mapped where recognized. Lithology is recorded primarily to distinguish geomorphic units formed from granitic parent rocks that weather to grus. Geomorphic units derived from grus have a distinct composition and texture, resulting in unique landforms and a unique soil profile. Lithology is also recorded for pediment units, erosional surfaces of uncertain age that are frequently associated with granitic rocks weathering to grus. A full list of geomorphic unit label descriptions is listed in table 1. Each geomorphic unit is discussed in detail under the appropriate heading in the Description of Map Units below.

Composite Unit Labels

Overlying Unit (/)

Surficial geologic units commonly exist as thin (<2 m) veneers resting on older units, including bedrock. In areas where this relation is mappable, both the units and their stratigraphic relation are identified with a compound unit label that includes a slash (/). The younger and older units are indicated before and after the slash, respectively. Thus, Qya/Qoa indicates an area where a veneer of young alluvial fan deposits overlies old alluvial fan deposits. Similarly, Qyag/fpg indicates an area where a veneer of young alluvial fan deposits composed of grus overlies felsic plutonic rock that weathers to grus.

Mixed Units (+)

It is common for extensive areas to be composed of a patchwork or interweaving of more than one geomorphic unit, wherein individual units are too small to record at the resolution of the map. In this case, the entire area is mapped as a single exposure, with two geomorphic unit names separated by a plus sign (+) and with the most common geomorphic unit listed first. For example, an incised alluvial channel usually contains a narrow thread of active units; the rest of the area consists of abandoned young alluvial bars, swales, and overbank deposits, moderately vegetated. These small, late Holocene, young alluvial units (Qyay) cannot be mapped individually at map scale. In this case, the entire channel is mapped and given a designation of Qyay+Qaa. As a general rule, the first unit listed covers >50% of the area, and the second covers <50%, but >20%. Units that cover <20% are generally ignored; no geomorphic unit is perfectly homogeneous, and we consider 20% to be a negligible amount.

Parent Lithology (-)

Unit labels for pediment units may include a dash (-), followed by the parent lithology. For example, Qpi-fp indicates a Quaternary pediment, incised, with a felsic plutonic lithology.

Combinations of Composite Labels

Occasionally it is informative to use multiple composite unit labels to accurately identify a unit, although we attempted to minimize this to reduce the complexity of the unit labels. Where multiple labels are used, the two units joined by a plus (+) sign are combined first. For instance the unit Qaae/Qaa+Qya indicates that a veneer of Qaae overlies the mixed unit Qaa+Qya. Similarly, Qia+Qya/Qoa indicates that a veneer composed of the mixed unit Qia+Qya overlies Qoa.

Table 1. System for generating composite unit names.

["+" means units are present in patches too small to map individually and dominant unit is listed first; "/" means the unit on left overlies unit on right; "-" is used only in conjunction with pediments to describe pediment lithology; {} braces indicate inclusion in the unit name is optional; blank entries indicate column is not applicable for a given row]

	age[1]	process[2]	sub-age	process/landform[3]	lithology[4]
Q	a,y,i,o	a,ae	{y,o}	{d^1}	{g}
Q	a,y,i,o	w,we	{y,o}	{d^1}	{g}
Q	a,y,i,o	v	{y,o}		{g}
Q	a,y,i,o	e,ea,ew	{y,o}	{r,d^2,s^1}	
Q	a,y,i,o	g	{y,o}	{s^2,w^1}	
Q		h		a,s^3	
Q	a,y,i,o	p^1		{f^1,s^4,w^2,c^1}	
Q	a,y,i,o	l		{c^2, f^2, g, s^5}	
Q		p^2		v,i,d^3	{-bedrock}
Q	y,i,o	m		{c^3}	
Q		v^2			

[1] a, active; y, young; i, intermediate; o, old

[2] a, alluvial; ae, mixed alluvial (dominant) and eolian; w, wash; we, mixed wash (dominant) and eolian; v^1, valley axis; e, eolian; ea, mixed eolian (dominant) and alluvial; ew, mixed eolian (dominant) and wash; g, groundwater discharge; h, hillslope; p^1, playa; l, lake; p^2, pediment; m, mass movement; v^2, volcanic deposit; ml, made land (anthropogenic);

[3] y, young; o, old

[4] d^1, debris flow (queried where not directly observed); r, ramp; d^2, dune; s^1, sheet; s^2, spring mound; w^1, wetlands; a, abundant; s^3, sparse; f^1, fringe; s^4, sandy; w^2, wet; c^1, crystal; c^2, coarse-grained; f^2, fine-grained ; g, gravelly ; s^5, well-sorted ; c^3, colluvium; v, veneer; i, incised; d^3, dissected; c^3, colluvial

[5] g, grus; bedrock, any bedrock, typically fp

This system of labeling Quaternary units is complicated, but informative. Although letters may repeat, their order and relation to each other makes the labels unambiguous. For example, Qap must refer to Quaternary active playa rather than Quaternary active pediment, because pediment units do not have an age designation. Similarly, a trailing "d" in a unit label is unambiguous. For example, Qaad must refer to areas of Quaternary active alluvial debris-flow deposits and Qaed must refer to areas of Quaternary active eolian dune deposits, because only alluvial deposits contain debris-flows and only eolian deposits contain dunes. By combining information on age, environment, and composition in the unit labels, the map user can quickly comprehend the overall character of a given unit without referring to the detailed unit description. Another advantage is the ability to create a large number of possible unit labels, (>180 unique labels). In addition, the unit labels can be combined (+, /, -) to create tens of thousands of unique unit labels. In the Newberry Springs quadrangle database, there are approximately 450 unique unit labels. This labeling system may at first seem excessive; however, including details of geologic age, environment, and lithology in the unit labels accurately describes the natural complexity of the geology.

How to Read the Composite Unit labels

It may be useful to apply the following guidelines when a map unit label is long and confusing:

1. Concentrate on the primary unit, initially ignoring any secondary units in the label; that is, any map unit listed after a "+", "/", or "-". For example, think of Qae/Qiaog as Qae.

2. Concentrate on the age and process (the first two or three letters after the Q). That is, ignore sub-age, sub-process, and lithology. If the map unit name is Qiayd, initially simplify it to Qia.

After the primary unit designation is understood, secondary information can be assimilated. If the user displays the database in a GIS, then the units can be simplified on the display as well by grouping and coloring them according to the above scheme. These guidelines should help the user navigate the map and database more efficiently. The user can then investigate the local subtleties recorded in the map unit label and in the database.

DESCRIPTION OF MAP UNITS

[Unit descriptions are listed in order of the following taxonomic features: (1) sediment grain size and roundness, color, and composition; (2) sedimentary structure and consolidation; (3) deposit surface morphology; (4) soil development; (5) inset relations with other units; (6) characteristic landforms and position in landscape, with particular attention to imagery; and (7) vegetation characteristics, and (or) any other diagnostic features. Primary categories are grouped by depositional transport process, with constituent units listed in order of increasing age. Nomenclature for calcic soil (K) horizons follows Gile and others (1966) and Machette (1985). Correlation of map units is shown on the map sheet.]

SURFICIAL DEPOSITS

ANTHROPOGENIC DEPOSITS

ml   **Modified land or artificial fill (latest Holocene)**—Natural or man-made materials emplaced for various purposes, including construction, agriculture, flood control, and mining. Also includes areas where surface sediments have been removed by grading or quarrying. Modified land typically alters patterns and rates of drainage, infiltration, soil erosion, and soil development. Sedimentary structures, surface morphology, and soils inherited from original deposit typically are altered or destroyed. Often visible on aerial photographs as simple geometric patterns and areas of consistent albedo, for example linear dark strips for roads and bright circles for crop patches. Vegetation is typically sparse and dominated by first-succession species

ALLUVIAL DEPOSITS

Qaa   **Active alluvial fan deposits (latest Holocene)**—Poorly to moderately sorted fine sand to boulders deposited by ephemeral streams that actively receive or have received sediments within the last few years or decades. Typically unconsolidated and uncemented, thus easily eroded. Surface undulates with rounded microtopography common to braided streams and pronounced bar and swale topography; incised channels are shallow or absent. Active fan channels originate from the mountain front, incised in the proximal fan and tending to diffuse in the distal fan; distinct from active washes (Qaw), which generally occur at the base of fans and trend parallel to the mountain front. Soil development is minimal but fine grained eolian sediment may be abundant, especially in distal piedmont areas. Surfaces are prone to flooding. Main proximal fan channels are sharply defined on aerial photographs as long, bright, sinuous features and grade down-fan into complex braided-channel networks. Vegetation typically reflects age of exposure, with recently active surfaces having sparse annuals, and older surfaces supporting a patchwork of shrubs such as creosote bush (*Larrea tridentata*) and white bursage (*Ambrosia dumosa*) on surfaces active only decadally

Qaag   **Active alluvial fan grus deposits (latest Holocene)**—Moderately sorted to well-sorted coarse sand to fine gravel derived from granitic sources that weather to grus. Sedimentary structures typically inconspicuous or lacking and surface morphology subdued. Active surface commonly inset less than 0.5 m into oldest alluvial deposits. Maximum clast size does not vary appreciably with distance from mountain front. Occurs in southwestern quadrant of map area

Qya   **Young alluvial fan deposits (Holocene and latest Pleistocene)**—Poorly to moderately sorted fine sand to boulders deposited by ephemeral streams; deposits have surfaces that have received little or no deposition in the last several thousand years. Poorly cemented: loose to slightly compact. Surfaces either permanently abandoned or flooded infrequently by channel avulsions in distributary streams at centennial to millennial intervals

Qyay   **Younger young alluvial fan deposits (Holocene)**—Microtopography fairly rough in much of fan consisting of remnants of bar-and-swale topography, with largest clasts concentrated in the elevated bars. No desert pavement. Poorly developed soil, expressed as incipient sandy A_v horizon; no significant B or C horizon development in soil profile. On aerial photographs shows as large areas of uniform, moderate albedo, with low-albedo speckling due to vegetation. Smaller patches show as moderate albedo areas between high-albedo active alluvial deposits and low-albedo desert pavements. Vegetation moderately abundant, typically including creosote bush (*Larrea tridentata*), and white bursage (*Ambrosia dumosa*). Less frequently, and at higher elevations, includes cheesebush (*Hymenoclea salsola*), ratany (*Krameria parvifolia*), Mojave yucca (*Yucca schidigera*), Mormon tea (*ephedra viridis*), and pencil, silver, and teddybear cholla (*Opuntia arbuscula, echinocarpa, and bigelovia*). Rodent burrows are ubiquitous throughout the map unit, especially around creosote bushes. Biological soil crusts locally dense, spanning several to tens of square meters, often concentrated near the edges separating Qyay-Qaa units

Qyad   **Young alluvial fan debris-flow deposits (Holocene and latest Pleistocene)**—Muddy sand containing scattered pebbles, cobbles, and boulders; poorly sorted and poorly stratified. Mainly deposited by debris

29

flows, but large-volume deposits may grade laterally or vertically into weakly stratified, moderately sorted hyperconcentrated stream deposits. Coarse levee deposits form where flows overtop banks. Flows may also divert streams by plugging channels. Difficult to distinguish from Qyay on aerial photographs; surfaces may appear slightly rougher on stereoscopic photo images. Mapped only where determined from field observations; hence more widespread than shown

Qyayd   **Younger young alluvial fan debris-flow deposits (Holocene)**—Deposit surfaces very rough, with steep-sided levees and depositional lobes. Coarse, boulder-sized particles are concentrated near surge fronts; interiors are also boulder-studded. Weak A_v horizon. Poorly vegetated. Deposits occur along mountain front northwest of Broadwell Lake

Qyag   **Young alluvial fan grus deposits (Holocene and latest Pleistocene)**— Moderately sorted to well-sorted coarse sand to fine gravel derived from granitic sources that weather to grus. Surface morphology undulating and smooth, with little dissection and minimal soil development. Maximum clast size does not vary appreciably with distance from mountain front. Especially common downslope of Early Proterozoic granitoids and associated pegmatites. Compared to unit Qya, there is less soil development and less incision near mountain fronts than unit Qyay

Qyayg   **Younger Young alluvial fan grus deposits (Holocene)**—Incipient A_v horizon, if present, is sandy. Lacks B and C horizon

Qyao   **Older young alluvial fan deposits (early Holocene and latest Pleistocene)**—Deposits have surfaces that have been primarily abandoned for the last ten thousand years, characterized by small patches of weakly to moderately developed pavement with slightly dark varnish. Soil profile has 1–4 cm thick A_v horizon, typically somewhat sandy, with a B_w horizon and stage I to II calcic development in C horizon. Deposits typically are incised by active deposits. Bar-and-swale topography moderately subdued, with flattened bars and incipient pavement in swales. Slightly dark varnish, resulting in moderate to moderately low albedo, may resemble slightly darkly varnished intermediate alluvial deposits but is typically dissected by a denser network of active alluvial channels. Moderately vegetated to well-vegetated, similar to Qyay. Dense biological soil crusts locally span several square meters

Qyaod   **Older young alluvial fan debris-flow deposits (early Holocene and latest Pleistocene)**—Soil profile consists of A_v horizon 1–4 cm thick, typically somewhat sandy; weak B_w horizon; and stage I to II calcic C horizon. Surfaces are moderately rough, with steep-sided levees and depositional lobes, but topography is somewhat subdued due to diffusive processes. Difficult to distinguish from Qyay on aerial photographs; sometimes displays slightly rougher textures in stereo. Mapped only where determined from field observations; deposits are much more widespread than shown

Qyaog   **Older young alluvial fan grus deposits (early Holocene and latest Pleistocene)**—Characterized by weakly developed pavements that generally lack varnish. Soil development is intermediate between Qyay and Qyao. A_v horizon is sandier and more weakly developed than Qyao, B_w horizon is poorly developed, and calcic horizon development is no greater than stage I to II

Qia **Intermediate alluvial fan deposits (late and middle Pleistocene)**—Poorly to moderately sorted fine sand to boulder gravel; deposits have surfaces that have been abandoned for tens to many tens of thousands of years. Clasts mostly subangular to subrounded, coarsening uphill toward mountain fronts. Deposits typically compact, but may be loose where bioturbated. Bar-and-swale topography replaced via diffusive processes with broad, flat, surfaces, that contain exposed clasts. Light grey-brown to dark brown depending on lithology and degree of varnish. Top of unit is incised by low to moderately dense channel networks; younger surfaces are locally inset along channel margin. Moderately to strongly developed desert pavement, with moderately dark to dark varnish. Underside of exposed clasts shows weak to strong rubification. Well-developed A_v horizon (>5 cm thick), composed of silt, very fine sand, and clay, with 2–5 cm platy peds. Pavement, varnish, and A_v horizon subdued to absent at altitudes above approximately 1,100 m; B_t horizon thicker and K horizon thinner at high elevation. Sparsely to moderately vegetated, abundance and species diversity increasing with elevation. Dominant species are creosote bush (*Larrea tridentata*) and white bursage (*Ambrosia dumosa*); also common are Mojave yucca (*Yucca chidigera*) and buckhorn cholla (*Opuntia acanthocarpa* var. *coloradensis*)

Qiay **Younger Intermediate alluvial fan deposits (late Pleistocene)**— Depositional surfaces that have been abandoned for tens of thousands of years. Geomorphic surfaces are incised by low to moderately dense channel networks, >2 m high in proximal fan environments, several centimeters or more in distal fan environments; younger surfaces are locally inset along channel margin. Moderately to strongly developed interlocking desert pavement with moderately dark to dark varnish on clasts. Underside of exposed clasts shows weak to strong rubification. Moderately to well developed B_t, B_{tk}, or B_{tq} horizon. Stage II to III+ carbonate accumulation in K horizon (locally may be as weak as stage I+ in areas of low carbonate influx). On aerial photographs appears as elongate, very low albedo patches of desert pavement cut by high-albedo active channels. Extensive bioturbation tends to inhibit pedogenesis at high elevations where black brush (*Coleogyne ramosissima*) is abundant; in such areas Qiay may be distinguished from younger deposits using alternate criteria, such as geomorphic position and weathering of surface clasts

Qiad **Intermediate alluvial fan debris-flow deposits (late and middle Pleistocene)**—Alluvial deposits dominated by debris flows; poorly sorted deposits consisting of boulders and smaller clasts encased in sand and silt matrix

Qiayd **Younger Intermediate alluvial fan debris-flow deposits (late Pleistocene)**—Sedimentologic characteristics similar to Qyad, but

31

pavement and soil profile similar to Qiay. Mapped only where verified by field observations, hence more widespread than shown

Qiag   **Intermediate alluvial fan grus deposits (late and middle Pleistocene)—** Coarse sandy to gravelly deposits derived from granitic sources that weather to grus. Surface broadly undulating, gently rounding downward into active alluvial deposits that form low to moderately dense channel networks cutting the surface. Although diagnostic inset relations are rare, exposed B horizons within inset younger channels denote the surface is being incised. In contrast to the general unit Qia, Qiag lacks or has a very weakly developed desert pavement, with no or slightly dark desert varnish. Underside of exposed clasts shows weak rubification. A_v horizon is sandy, B_t horizon is moderately to well developed

Qiayg   **Younger Intermediate alluvial fan grus deposits (late Pleistocene)—** Moderately-developed B horizon (B_w or B_t). Carbonate accumulation in the K horizon is stage I to II

Qiao   **Older Intermediate alluvial fan deposits (late to middle Pleistocene)—** Depositional surfaces that have been abandoned for many tens of thousands of years. Geomorphic surfaces are flat and smooth, with edges rounded by diffusive processes; incised >3 m by low-density channel networks in proximal fan environments; generally not present in distal fan environments. Strongly developed interlocking desert pavement, with moderately dark to dark varnish on clasts; locally degraded by diffusive or other processes. Underside of exposed clasts shows strong rubification. A_v horizon may be thin or nonexistent in patches, where pavement has degraded and the A_v horizon has been stripped, exposing the B horizon. Well-developed B_{tk} or B_{tq} horizon. Stage III to IV carbonate accumulation in K horizon. On aerial photographs appears mottled, with elongate, low to moderately low albedo patches of desert pavement dotted with high-albedo disturbed areas surrounding vegetation and rodent burrows, and cut by high-albedo active channels. Vegetation is moderately abundant and increases with elevation; maximum densities occur at the beveled edges of active channels and in disturbed areas

Qiaog   **Older Intermediate alluvial fan grus deposits (late and middle Pleistocene)—**Surface generally broader, with channel networks less dense than Qiayg. B horizon generally more developed than Qiayg (B_t). Carbonate accumulation in the K horizon is stage II to II+

Qoa   **Old alluvial fan deposits (middle and early Pleistocene)—**Poorly to moderately sorted fine sand to boulders; deposits have surfaces that have been abandoned for several hundred thousand years. Clasts mostly subangular to subrounded, coarsening uphill toward mountain fronts. Clasts on surface commonly include disaggregated pieces of the petrocalcic soil K horizon. Compact and cemented near surface. Commonly forms pale-colored, broad, round-topped, deeply dissected ridges (ballenas of Peterson, 1981) standing a few meters to tens of meters above active washes in the proximal alluvial fan environment; little or no remnant depositional geomorphology. Original upper soil horizons are largely eroded, but locally younger soils may be superimposed directly on well-developed K horizon (calcium accumulation stage ≥IV). These younger soils may include remnant desert pavement, with darkly varnished clasts and accompanying fragments of calcic K horizon at the surface, overlying a very thin or absent B_t horizon. Calcium accumulation in the K horizon ≥stage IV and 2 to 6 m thick. In aerial photographs appears mottled, with moderate to low-albedo surfaces of degraded desert pavement and incipient soils interrupted by high-albedo patches of exposed petrocalcic horizon, where pavement or degraded pavement stones are mixed with exposed fragments of weathered, high-albedo petrocalcic horizon material. In general, these mottled areas are not extensive, forming somewhat isolated surfaces near mountain fronts. Moderately vegetated

Qoag   **Old alluvial fan grus deposits (middle and early Pleistocene)**—Coarse sandy deposits derived from granitic source that weathers to grus; texture and detrital composition similar to Qyaog. Upper parts of soil profile including A_v and B_t horizons are commonly eroded, exposing K horizon. Calcic accumulation typically stage IV. More deeply incised than unit Qiag. Albedo generally high due to granitic parent material and abundant pedogenic carbonate

QToa   **Extremely old Quaternary-Tertiary alluvial fan deposit (early Pleistocene and Pliocene)**—Poorly to moderately sorted, boulder-bearing deposits composed of silt, sand, gravel, and cobbles; deposits have surfaces that have been abandoned for hundreds of thousands of years. Compact and locally cemented. Forms deeply dissected, rugged, terrain with little or no remnant depositional landforms. Paleocurrent trend and detrital provenance generally inconsistent with modern topography and drainage network. Several sets of paleosols commonly exposed in cross-cutting washes. Younger, superimposed, soil horizons locally present. Less consolidated and cemented than unit pc. Precise age generally not determined. Along the northwestern edge of the Newberry Mountains accordant, rounded ridgecrests are locally preserved and seem to be remnants of the original depositional top of the unit

QToag   **Extremely old alluvial fan grus deposits (early Pleistocene to Tertiary)**—Coarse sandy deposits derived from granitic source that weathers to grus; texture and detrital composition similar to Qyaog

WASH DEPOSITS AND MOJAVE RIVER WASH DEPOSITS

Qaw   **Active wash deposit (latest Holocene)**—Moderately to poorly sorted, fine sand
QawMR   to boulder gravel deposited by ephemeral streams that actively receive or have received sediments within the last few decades. Similar in character to unit Qaa but generally better sorted and stratified. Typically forms wider, longer, more gently sloping channels that drain small inter-fan valleys; thus flows more frequently than alluvial fan channels. Deposits loose and unconsolidated, easily disturbed. No soil development. As much as several meters of active sediments commonly have accumulated within the past few decades. Appears on aerial photographs as long,

bright, somewhat sinuous features trending perpendicular to the base of distal fans. Recently active surfaces contain sparse vegetation, commonly including Smoke Tree (*Dalea Spinosa*) and Mesquite (*Prosopis Pubescens*). Channels active at decadal intervals are moderately vegetated on surfaces or with desert senna (*Senna Armata*), cheesebush (*Hymenoclea salsola*), and catsclaw (*Acacia greggii* var. *arizonica*). Active wash deposits that drain the Mojave River are designated QawMR to indicate Mojave River sediment and fluvial system. The Mojave River subunit is distinguished by predominance of grus with admixture of fine pebbles of quartzite and volcanic rocks. Sandy deposits occupy the broad channel of the Mojave River and are interbedded with muddy sediments in bordering floodplain areas. Willows, cottonwoods, and other phreatophytes are common, especially where fault zones or shallow bedrock force groundwater nearly to the land surface

Qyw
QywMR

Young wash deposits (Holocene and latest Pleistocene)—Poorly to moderately sorted, mixed clastic sediment ranging from fine sand to boulders; deposits have surfaces that have been abandoned for several thousand years. Poorly cemented and poorly consolidated. Loose to slightly compact. Surfaces largely inactive, forming terraces above active wash surfaces. Vegetation commonly includes creosote bush (*Larrea tridentata*) and white bursage (*Ambrosia dumosa*), cheesebush (*Hymenoclea salsola*), ratany (*Krameria parvifolia*), Mormon tea (*ephedra viridis*) and rabbitbrush (*Chrysothamnus nauseosus*). Locally designated QywMR to indicate undivided young wash deposits of the Mojave River, which are grusy like Qywg, but also contain small pebbles of quartzite and volcanic rocks

Qywy
QywyMR
Qywyg

Younger young wash deposit (Holocene)—Wash deposits characterized by surfaces that have been abandoned or receive materials very infrequently. Commonly contains remnants of bar and swale topography. No desert pavement. Incipient to slightly dark varnish on clasts. Poorly developed soil, expressed as incipient to weak sandy A_v horizon and weak B_w horizon; calcic horizon absent or stage I. Forms wide channels, concentrating drainage from, and roughly perpendicular to, local alluvial fan drainages. On aerial photographs appears as large areas of uniform, moderate albedo, with low-albedo speckling due to vegetation. Abundant vegetation. Rodent burrows are common, but less so than for Qyay. Unit is similar to Qyay, but occurs in washes in the inter-fan environment. Qywyg is similar to Qywy, but consists of sediments containing abundant granules derived from granitic source rocks weathering to grus. QywyMR indicates grusy Mojave River deposits. Deposits border the broad channel of the Mojave River, typically forming terraces 1.5 to 2 m higher than the active channel. Moderate plant cover commonly includes creosote bush (*Larrea tridentata*) and saltbush (*Atriplex* spp.)

Qywo
QywoMR

Older young wash deposits (Early Holocene and latest Pleistocene)— Wash deposits characterized by small patches of weakly to moderately developed desert pavement with slightly dark varnish. A_v horizon 1 to 4

34

cm thick and typically somewhat sandy, weak B_w horizon and stage I to II calcic development in K horizon. Deposits are typically inset into intermediated deposits and incised by active channels. Surface has moderate to subdued bar-and-swale topography and shows an overall flattening, with desert pavement developing in swales. On aerial photographs, appears as moderate to moderately low albedo patches; intermediate alluvial deposits with slightly dark varnish may appear similar, but are cut by fewer actively incising channels. Moderately vegetated to well-vegetated. Dense biological soil crusts locally span several square meters. Very similar to Qyao, but occurs in washes in the inter-fan environment. Locally designated QywoMR to indicate grusy Mojave River deposits. Forms wide plain extending from Daggett east to Newberry Springs and Manix Wash. Deposits exposed in banks of Mojave River include well-stratified, moderately sorted channel gravel, poorly sorted sandy crevasse splay deposits, muddy to finely sandy floodplain deposits, and muddy marsh deposits with organic materials and groundwater-discharge carbonate blebs. Surface of the plain is undulatory and has inverted topography, with high areas consisting of anastamosing former gravel-filled channels, which have been exposed by erosion of finer-grained sediments. Terraces locally inset about 1.5 m below top of unit apparently represent a slightly younger deposit

Qiw
QiwMR **Intermediate wash deposits (late and middle Pleistocene)**—Poorly to moderately sorted fine sand to boulder gravel; deposits have surfaces that have been abandoned for tens to many tens of thousands of years. Clasts mostly subangular to subrounded, coarsening uphill toward mountain fronts. Deposits typically compact, but may be loose where bioturbated. Bar-and-swale topography replaced via diffusive processes with broad, flat, surfaces, that have light grey-brown to dark brown exposed clasts, depending on lithology and degree of varnish. Unit is similar to Qia, but occurs in washes in the inter-fan environment. Top of unit is incised by low to moderately dense channel networks; younger surfaces are locally inset along channel margin. Moderately to strongly developed desert pavement, with moderately dark to dark varnish. Underside of exposed clasts shows weak to strong rubification. Well-developed A_v horizon (>5 cm thick), composed of silt, very fine sand, and clay, with 2–5 cm platy peds. Pavement, varnish, and A_v horizon subdued to absent at altitudes above approximately 1,100 m; B_t horizon thicker and K horizon thinner at high elevation. Sparsely to moderately vegetated; abundance and species diversity increasing with elevation. Dominant species are creosote bush (*Larrea tridentata*) and white bursage (*Ambrosia dumosa*); also common are Mojave yucca (*Yucca chidigera*) and buckhorn cholla (*Opuntia acanthocarpa* var. *coloradensis*).

Locally designated QiwMR to indicate grusy Mojave River deposits. Deposits occur in several locations north of the Mojave River, where deposit is uplifted and deformed by folds and minor thrust faults

Qiwy **Intermediate young wash deposits (late Pleistocene)**—Depositional surfaces that have been abandoned for tens of thousands of years.

Typically forms elongate, flat surfaces, abandoned and incised >2 m on all sides in inter-fan channelized wash settings, several centimeters or more in diffuse-runoff wash settings; younger surfaces are locally inset along channel margin. Moderately to strongly developed interlocking desert pavement with moderately dark to dark varnish on clasts. Underside of exposed clasts shows weak to strong rubification. Moderately to well developed B_t, B_{tk}, or B_{tq} horizon. Stage II to III+ carbonate accumulation in K horizon (locally may be as weak as stage I+ in areas of low carbonate influx). On aerial photographs appears as elongate, very low albedo patches of desert pavement cut by high-albedo active channels

EOLIAN DEPOSITS

Qae **Active eolian sand deposits (latest Holocene)**—Light to gray, pale-brown, moderately sorted to well-sorted fine to medium sand; moderately cross laminated, containing few clasts. Loose and subject to migration. Gently sloping topography; gradational contacts with neighboring units. No soil development. On aerial photography has high-albedo. Generally lacks vegetation, but some undifferentiated units low (<0.5 m) shrub mounds

Qaed **Active eolian sand dune deposits (latest Holocene)**—Light to gray, pale-brown, moderately sorted to well-sorted fine to medium sand. Similar to unit Qae, but has pronounced dune morphology

Qaer **Active eolian sand ramp deposits (latest Holocene)**—Ramp of inclined sand sheets or wedge-shaped sand deposits on windward or lee side of mountains or hills (climbing and falling dunes). Deposits typically occur near local sand sources such as playas or playa fringes

Qaes **Active eolian sand sheet deposits (latest Holocene)**—Silt and fine to coarse sand; forms sheets and low dunes covering gently inclined bedrock surfaces. Sand fills large cracks and joints on the bedrock surface allowing deep-rooted vegetation to develop. Located along the fringes of the Pisgah volcanic field. Sand-sheet veneer deposits are widespread and common through the map area but most are too thin and small to show. No soil development. High-albedo on aerial photography. Contacts with neighboring units are typically gradational

Qye **Young eolian sand deposits (Holocene and latest Pleistocene)**—Pale brown, moderately sorted to well-sorted, fine- to medium-sand deposits. Moderately cross-laminated, containing few clasts. Loose to slightly compacted. Surfaces of deposits are typically inactive. On aerial photographs has slightly darker albedo than unit Qae. Sparsely vegetated

Qyed **Young eolian sand dune deposits (Holocene and latest Pleistocene)**—Dune deposits, locally including coppice dunes. Commonly strongly cross-laminated. Steep, with lee and stoss slopes poorly to moderately well defined. Deposits are common on west side of Troy Lake, likely sourced locally from the Mojave River channel

MIXED EOLIAN AND ALLUVIAL DEPOSITS

Qaea   **Active mixed eolian and alluvial deposits (latest Holocene)**—Active eolian sand interstratified with lenses of alluvial fan deposits. Lithologically and morphologically similar to unit Qae, mainly consisting of loose, fine to medium sand with faintly defined to well-defined, thin cross bedding. Alluvial channels indistinct; deposit mostly sand with sparse gravel. Forms broad, flat surfaces actively migrating via sediment transport. Generally found in distal fan environment. No soil development. Sparsely vegetated, mainly with grasses; generally lacks creosote bush (*Larrea tridentata*). Mainly restricted to areas east of Troy Lake and east of Pisgah basalt flow south of I–40. Gradational contacts with neighboring units

Qaae   **Active mixed alluvial and eolian sand deposits (latest Holocene)**—Active alluvial fan deposits interstratified with lesser amounts of eolian sand. Lithologically and morphologically similar to unit Qaa, mainly consisting of loose gravelly sand with faintly defined to well-defined thin bedding. Active deposition of eolian sand is secondary but present throughout deposit. Sparse coppice mounds and small dunes, locally producing hummocky terrain. No soil development. High-albedo on aerial photographs. Sparse vegetation, commonly creosote bush (*Larrea tridentata*) and white bursage (*Ambrosia dumosa*) on surfaces active only decadally. Contacts with neighboring units are typically gradational

Qawe   **Active mixed wash and eolian sand deposits (latest Holocene)**—Moderately sorted to well-sorted, fine to medium sand with lenses of coarser gravelly sand to cobbles deposited by alluvial processes. Actively receives or has received sediments within the last few decades. Similar in character to unit Qaae, but generally better sorted and stratified. Typically forms wider, longer, more gently sloping channels that drain small inter-fan valleys; thus flows more frequently than alluvial fan channels. Deposits loose and unconsolidated, easily disturbed. Coppice mounds and small dunes present, but not dominant depositional landforms. No soil development. Appears on aerial photographs as long, bright, somewhat sinuous features trending perpendicular to the base of distal fans. Recently active surfaces contain sparse vegetation, commonly including smoke tree (*Dalea spinosa*) and mesquite (*Prosopis pubescens*). Channels active at decadal intervals are moderately vegetated on surfaces or with desert senna (*Senna armata*), cheesebush (*Hymenoclea salsola*), and catsclaw (*Acacia greggii* var. *arizonica*). Contacts with neighboring units are typically gradational

Qyea   **Young mixed eolian and alluvial deposits (Holocene and latest Pleistocene)**—Young deposits of eolian sand interstratified with lenses of alluvial fan deposits. Lithologically and morphologically similar to unit Qye, mainly consisting of loose, fine to medium sand with faintly defined to well-defined, thin cross bedding; sparse gravel. Forms broad, undulating surfaces with indistinct bar-and-swale topography. Prone to surface modification by eolian sediment transport. Generally occurs in distal fan environment. Soil development absent to poorly developed. On aerial photographs appears slightly less bright than unit Qye. Sparsely vegetated, mainly with grasses; generally lacks creosote bush (*Larrea tridentata*). Gradational contacts with neighboring units

Qyeay   **Younger young mixed eolian sand and alluvial deposits (Holocene)**— Deposit surfaces are abandoned or receive materials infrequently. Lithologically and morphologically similar to unit Qye with secondary alluvial deposits. Little or no soil development. Typically located southeast of playas in the map area

Qyeag   **Young mixed eolian sand and alluvial grus deposits (Holocene)**—Mixed deposits similar to unit Qyea, but containing coarse sand and pebbles derived from granitic rocks that weather to grus; granitic clasts and granules commonly litter surface

Qyae   **Young mixed alluvial and eolian sand deposits (Holocene and latest Pleistocene)**—Young alluvial fan deposits interstratified with lesser amounts of eolian sand. Lithologically and morphologically similar to unit Qya, consisting of loose to moderately compact gravelly sand with faintly defined to well-defined thin bedding. Forms broad, undulating surfaces with subdued bar-and-swale topography. Soil development absent to poorly developed, with sand A_v horizon and B_w horizon. On aerial photographs appears slightly darker than Qae surfaces. Moderately vegetated, generally supporting creosote bush (*Larrea tridentata*) and white bursage (*Ambrosia dumosa*). Contacts with neighboring units are typically gradational

Qyaey   **Younger young mixed alluvial and eolian sand deposits (Holocene)**— Loose sand and gravelly sand. Soil development absent or incipient. Sandy A_v horizon, if present, is 0.5–1 cm below active surface

Qyaeg   **Young mixed alluvial grus and eolian sand deposits (Holocene)**—Mixed deposits similar to unit Qyae, but containing coarse sand and pebbles derived from granitic rocks that weather to grus; granitic clasts and granules commonly litter surface

Qywey   **Younger young mixed wash and eolian sand deposits (Holocene)**—Poorly to moderately sorted mixed clastic sediment ranging from fine sand to boulders interstratified with lesser amounts of fine to medium, thinly bedded eolian sand deposits. Deposit surfaces have not received alluvial deposition for several thousand years. Typically forms wider, longer, more gently sloping units adjacent to channels that drain small inter-fan valleys. Loose and unconsolidated, easily disturbed. Forms broad, undulating surfaces with subdued bar-and-swale topography. Little or no soil development. Sandy A_v horizon, if present, contains significant sand and is ½ to 1 cm below active surface, and can extend to depths of >10 cm. On aerial photographs appears slightly darker than unit Qawe; landforms are less distinct. Moderately vegetated, typically supporting creosote bush (*Larrea tridentata*) and white bursage (*Ambrosia dumosa*). Contacts with neighboring units are gradational

Qyewy   **Young younger mixed eolian sand and wash deposits (Holocene)**—Fine to medium sand with faintly visible to well-defined thin bedding, interstratified with lenses of moderately sorted coarse sand to cobbles.

Loose; prone to surface modification by eolian sediment transport. Forms broad, undulating surfaces with indistinct bar-and-swale topography. Forms adjacent to wide channels roughly perpendicular to local alluvial fan drainages. Soil development absent to poorly developed. On aerial photographs appears slightly less bright than unit Qye. Sparsely vegetated, mainly with grasses; generally lacks creosote bush (*Larrea tridentata*). Gradational contacts with neighboring units

Qyeao **Older young mixed eolian sand and alluvial deposits (early Holocene and latest Pleistocene)**—No soil development to weak sandy A_v horizon; poorly developed B_w typically with stage I calcic development. Located east of Mojave River in Cady Mountains

Qyaeo **Older young mixed alluvial and eolian sand deposits (early Holocene and latest Pleistocene)**—Moderately compact sand and gravelly sand. Soil development retarded compared to unit Qyao. Sandy A_v horizon ~1 cm thick and 0.5–1 cm below the surface. May have B_w horizon. Surface has patches of incipient pavement with noninterlocking stones. Deposits are typically inset into intermediate deposits and incised by active deposits. On aerial photographs may appear slightly darker than unit Qyaey

Qiea **Intermediate mixed eolian sand and alluvial deposits (late and middle Pleistocene)**—Moderately sorted to well-sorted sand with minor lenses of poorly sorted to moderately sorted silt, gravel, cobbles. Surface composed of moderately sorted to well-sorted sand with dispersed subangular to subrounded clasts that coarsen in size toward mountain fronts. Somewhat loose from accumulation of eolian sand. Alluvial deposition on surfaces abandoned for tens to many tens of thousands of years; flattened by diffusive processes and devoid of bar and swale topography. Partly incised by narrow channels, with younger surfaces inset into the edges. Moderately to weakly developed patches of noninterlocking desert pavement with slightly dark to moderately dark varnish on clasts and sand in the interstices between pavement stones. Moderately developed to well developed soil profile. Appears as elongate, moderate-albedo patches of sandy desert pavement cut by active channels. Moderately vegetated, typically supporting creosote bush (*Larrea tridentata*) and white bursage (*Ambrosia dumosa*). Contacts with neighboring units are typically gradational

Qieay **Younger Intermediate mixed eolian sand and alluvial deposits (latest Pleistocene)**—Deposit surfaces abandoned by alluvial deposition for thousands of years. Typically incised by channels, >2 m in height in proximal fan environments, several centimeters in distal fan environments. A_v horizon contains significant sand, has subdued peds, and is commonly 0.5 cm below the active surface. Well-developed, sandy B_w or B_{wk} horizon. Stage I+ to II+ carbonate accumulation in K horizon. Occurs in the northern Bristol Mountains, south of mesquite playa

Qiae **Intermediate mixed alluvial and eolian sand deposits (late to middle Pleistocene)**—Intermediate alluvial fan deposits interstratified with lesser amounts of eolian sand. Poorly to moderately sorted mixtures of silt, gravel, cobbles, and boulders, interstratified with moderately sorted to well-sorted sand. Outcrop surfaces light grey-brown, shade varying with sediment composition and thickness of varnish. Clasts mostly subangular to subrounded, and coarser toward mountain fronts. Typically compact, but can be somewhat loose from influx of eolian sand. Lithologically and morphologically similar to unit Qia, with the addition of eolian sand throughout deposit. Sparse coppice mounds and small dunes, locally producing hummocky terrain. Channel density is low to moderate, incised, with younger surfaces inset into the edges. Moderately developed to well-developed soil profile, with sandy A_v, B_t and B_{tk}. Calcic accumulation in the K horizon stage I+ to IV. High-albedo on aerial photographs. Moderately vegetated, generally supporting creosote bush (*Larrea tridentata*) and white bursage (*Ambrosia dumosa*). Contacts with neighboring units are typically gradational

Qiaey   **Younger Intermediate mixed alluvial and eolian deposits (late Pleistocene)**—Characterized by surfaces abandoned for tens of thousands of years; flattened by diffusive processes and devoid of bar and swale topography. Moderately to weakly developed, noninterlocking desert pavement with slightly dark to moderately dark varnish on clasts and sand in the interstices between pavement stones. Forms flat smooth surfaces, incised by narrow channels that are often partly filled with eolian sand. Moderately developed to well-developed, sandy A_v horizon (>5 cm thick), commonly 0.5 cm below the active surface, has weak peds and is composed of fine sand, silt, and clay. Moderately developed, sandy B_t or B_{tk} horizon. Stage I+ to II+ calcic accumulation in K horizon. On aerial photographs appears as elongate, moderately low to moderate albedo patches of sandy desert pavement cut by high-albedo active channels

Qiaeg   **Intermediate mixed alluvial grus and eolian deposit (late and middle Pleistocene)**—Mixed deposits similar to unit Qiae, but containing coarse sand and pebbles derived from granitic rocks that weather to grus; granitic clasts and granules commonly litter surface. Forms flat surfaces in the distal fan zone adjacent to valley axis deposits that are the main source of eolian sediment. Pedogenesis is irregular and may be expressed by variably developed pavement and varnish, B_t horizon, and calcic horizon. Pavement surfaces are locally composed of ventifacts. Moderate to sparse vegetation. Exposures are limited to area downgradient from granitic source rocks of the Cady Mountains

Qiwey   **Younger Intermediate mixed wash and eolian sand deposits (late Pleistocene)**—Poorly to moderately sorted silt, gravel, cobbles, and boulders, interstratified with lenses of fine to medium, thinly bedded eolian sand deposits. Surface composed of moderately sorted to well-sorted sand with dispersed subangular to subrounded clasts. Somewhat loose from accumulation of eolian sand. Alluvial deposition on surfaces abandoned for tens of thousands of years, flattened by diffusive

40

processes, and devoid of bar-and-swale topography. Typically forms wider, longer, more gently sloping units in inter-fan valleys. Incised >1 m by narrow channels, with younger surfaces inset into the edges. Moderately to weakly developed, noninterlocking desert pavement with slightly dark to moderately dark varnish on clasts, and sand in the interstices between pavement stones (fig. 13). Moderately developed to well-developed, sandy A_v horizon (>5 cm thick) with subdued peds, composed of fine sand, silt, and clay, commonly 0.5 cm below the active surface. Poorly to moderately developed, sandy B_w, B_t or B_{tk} horizon. Stage I+ to II+ carbonate accumulation in K horizon. On aerial photographs appears as somewhat elongate, moderately low to moderate-albedo patches of sandy desert pavement cut by high-albedo active channels. Moderately vegetated, typically supporting creosote bush (*Larrea tridentata*) and white bursage (*Ambrosia dumosa*) (fig. 13). Contacts with neighboring units are typically gradational

Qieao **Older Intermediate mixed eolian sand and alluvial deposits (late and middle Pleistocene)**—Deposit surfaces abandoned by alluvial deposition for tens of thousands of years. Typically incised several meters by channels. Generally proximal to mountain fronts. Thin to absent, sandy A_v horizon covers well-developed, sandy B_w or B_{wk} horizon. Stage III to III+ carbonate accumulation in K horizon. Occurs in the northeastern Bristol mountains

Qiaeo **Older Intermediate mixed alluvial and eolian sand deposits (late and middle Pleistocene)**—Characterized by surfaces that have been abandoned for many tens of thousands of years. Noninterlocking, degraded desert pavement has moderately dark varnish on clasts. Forms flat, smooth surfaces with beveled edges, incised by narrow channels. Deposits tend to be more deeply incised than Qiaey. Well-developed, sandy A_v horizon (>5 cm thick), composed of sand, silt, and clay. A_v horizon often thin or nonexistent in patches where pavement is degraded and A_v horizon has been stripped, exposing the B_t horizon. Moderately developed to well-developed B_t or B_{tk} horizon. Stage III to IV carbonate accumulation in K horizon. On aerial photographs appears as elongate and mottled, with moderately low to moderate albedo patches of desert pavement cut by high-albedo active channels. Mottling on desert pavement due to higher-albedo spots from vegetation and rodent burrows. Moderately vegetated, especially at the beveled edges near active channels and in disturbed areas, with creosote bush (*Larrea tridentata*) and white bursage (*Ambrosia dumosa*)

Qoae **Old mixed alluvial and eolian sand deposits (middle and early Pleistocene)**—Old alluvial fan deposits interstratified with lesser amounts of eolian sand. Poorly to moderately sorted mixtures of silt, gravel, cobbles, and boulders, interstratified with moderately sorted to well-sorted sand. Moderately compact. Lithologically and morphologically similar to unit Qoa, with the addition of eolian sand throughout deposit. Forms flat surfaces. Location not necessarily correlated with modern source of eolian sediment. Pedogenesis less developed than unit Qoa; inconsistently developed pavement and varnish, B_t horizon, and calcic accumulation in K horizon. Pavement surfaces may be composed of ventifacts. Moderate to sparse vegetation, supporting creosote bush (*Larrea tridentata*) and white bursage (*Ambrosia dumosa*)

PLAYA DEPOSITS

Qap   **Active playa deposits (latest Holocene)**—Weakly bedded, poorly sorted, compact silt, clay, and sand; locally salt rich. Forms broad, extensive, very flat floors of ephemeral lakes and ponds that have received water and sediment from surrounding source areas within the past few decades. Deposits have undergone seasonal flooding and drying cycles, with associated sediment expansion and shrinkage; locally may also show displacive growth of salt crystals. Subject to eolian deposition and erosion. Thin to thick subhorizontal bedding. Mud-cracked; may have linear fissures or mounds that support vegetation. High to very high-albedo in aerial photographs. Generally lacks or has sparse vegetation. In Broadwell Lake, fissures form accretionary ridges that support white bursage (*Ambrosia dumosa*)

Qaps   **Active playa sandy facies**— Sandy facies of playa that typically supports sparse vegetation, generally near margin of playa where alluvial sediments interfinger with playa sediments

Qapf   **Active playa fringe deposits (latest Holocene)**—Poorly sorted to moderately sorted sand and silt, with minor amounts of cobbles, gravel, and clay. Loose and unconsolidated. Surface is undulating, with indistinct bar-and-swale topography. Prone to frequent surface modification by eolian sediment transport; less frequent flooding and alluvial deposition. May have groundwater-discharge deposits or salts. No soil development. High-albedo on aerial photography. Vegetation dominated by grasses, with few shrubs and accompanying coppice mounds

Qyp   **Young playa deposits (Holocene and latest Pleistocene)**—Fine sand and silt to sandy clay. Deposits are typically capped by a weakly cemented, massive sand crust overlying several centimeters of loose sand and silt and a deeper layer of moderately compact sand and silt cemented with gypsum. Surfaces irregular; commonly incised by local drainages and has coppice mounds of eolian sand as much as 1 m high. Vegetation sparse, includes desert holly (*Chenopodiaceae*) and local annuals

Qypf   **Young playa fringe deposits (Holocene and latest Pleistocene)**—Poorly sorted to moderately sorted sand and silt, with minor amounts of cobbles, gravel, and clay. Loose and unconsolidated. Surface is undulating, with indistinct bar-and-swale topography. Has not received flooding or alluvial deposition in thousands of years. Prone to frequent surface modification by eolian sediment transport. Minor dissection of surface by stream channels. Little to no soil development. High-albedo on aerial photography. Moderately well vegetated; typically supporting grass and sparse creosote bush (*Larrea tridentata*).

Qypof   **Older young playa fringe deposit (Holocene and latest Pleistocene)**—Pale brown to light gray, clay, silt, sand, and tufa deposits. Complexly mixed material of eolian, lacustrine, playa, alluvial, and groundwater-discharge origin; includes tufa mounds. Similar to Qypf deposits, but more elevated and dissected and locally preserves B_w–B_t soil horizon. Mapped in southwest corner of quadrangle adjacent to younger Qyp and Qypf deposits of Lucerne Lake

QTop   **Extremely old playa-lacustrine and alluvial deposits (early Pleistocene and Pliocene)**—Moderately indurated to well-indurated clayey silt to fine to medium sand. Contains thin interbeds of gray-green silt and white to pale-gray volcanic ash; locally gypsiferous. Forms badlands topography. Sparse vegetation, includes saltbush (*Atriplex*). Exposed along the Mojave River from near mouth of Manix Wash northeastward to northern border of map area. Nagy and Murray (1991, 1996) described these Pliocene-Pleistocene deposits in detail and informally named them the Mojave River formation

AXIAL VALLEY DEPOSITS

Qav   **Active axial valley deposits (latest Holocene)**—Moderately to poorly sorted fine gravel, sand, silt, and clay deposited by ephemeral axial valley streams that actively receive or have received sediments within the last few decades. Prone to flooding. Loose and easily disturbed. Forms anastomosing washes and rounded interfluves, and commonly interfingers with eolian sediments. Channel generally follows regional topographic gradient and diverges from gradients of local alluvial fans. Channels are typically at least several meters wide and carry more runoff than channels of active alluvial (Qaa) and wash (Qaw) channels. Little or no soil development. On aerial photographs appears as long, sinuous, high-albedo strands. Sparsely to moderately vegetated with creosote bush (*Larrea tridentata*), cheesebush (*Hymenoclea salsola*), and black-banded rabbitbrush (*Chrysothamnus paniculatus*)

Qyv   **Young axial valley deposits (Holocene and latest Pleistocene)**—Moderately to poorly sorted sand, silt, and clay. Occasionally flooded. Loose to somewhat consolidated. Forms anastomosing washes and associated low-sloping interfluves and commonly inter-fingers with eolian sediments. Poorly developed soil, expressed as incipient to weak sandy A_v horizon and poorly developed B_w horizon; calcic accumulation in K horizon absent or restricted to stage I. Moderately vegetated

Qyvo   **Older young axial valley deposits (early Holocene and latest Pleistocene)**—Poorly to moderately developed soil, consisting of incipient to weak sandy A_v horizon and poorly to moderately developed B_w horizon; calcic accumulation in K horizon absent or restricted to stage I. Located west of Troy Lake along I–40

Qiv   **Intermediate axial valley deposits (late and middle Pleistocene)**—Medium to fine sand to silt and clay, interbedded with coarse sand and gravel. Generally very pale brown to light yellow, but coarse sand and gravel may be darker. Moderately to deeply dissected deposits located in the inactive valley axes. Locally consists of interbedded alluvial, eolian, and groundwater-discharge deposits. On aerial photographs appears light gray to white and in Landsat imagery appears very pale brown to medium brown

GROUNDWATER DISCHARGE DEPOSITS

Qag   **Active groundwater-discharge deposits (latest Holocene)**—Poorly to well consolidated, white, gray, and very pale brown calcareous, siliceous, and gypsiferous deposits; slightly domal, lacking identifiable spring craters. Commonly contains minor amounts of eolian sand or silt and finely disseminated organic matter. Authigenic gypsum generally consists of scattered, sand-sized lenticular grains set in a cryptocrystalline matrix. Cylindrical casts and molds derived from the roots and stems of in-situ plants are locally abundant. Deposits overlie valley floor alluvium and (or) bedrock. Locally disturbed by small-scale historic mining exploration

Qagw   **Active groundwater-discharge wetland deposits (latest Holocene)**— Well-bedded, massive silt and clay. Forms broad, flat deposits. Nodular calcite in sediments. Often has algal mats. Well vegetated.

Qyg   **Young groundwater-discharge deposits (Holocene and latest Pleistocene)**— Silt and fine sand in zones of former groundwater-discharge, generally calcareous. Loose to compact. May have rhizoliths, ostracode fossils, and charophyte fossils. Commonly forms light-colored, flat areas or dissected badlands. In aerial photographs has high-albedo

Qygw   **Young groundwater-discharge wetland deposits (Holocene and latest Pleistocene)**—Generally similar to unit Qyg, but forms broad, low relief landforms. South of the Ord Mountains deposits, inset into Qia deposits and, in turn, cut by middle Holocene unit Qyay, in association with faults

Qygs   **Young groundwater-discharge spring mound deposits (Holocene and latest Pleistocene)**—Generally similar to unit Qyg, but has distinct mound landforms that commonly rise 1–2 m above adjacent deposits. Occurs in association with eolian and playa fringe deposits. Observed north of the Pisgah basalt flow to the west of the Pisgah Fault and as northwest-trending mounds associated with the Pisgah Fault near Hector

Qig   **Intermediate groundwater-discharge deposits (late and middle Pleistocene)**—Silt and fine sand in former zones of groundwater-discharge; source processes unidentified. Generally white to light brown; compact. Contains one or more stage III to IV pedogenic calcic horizons. Little vegetation, generally dissected

Qigw   **Intermediate groundwater-discharge wetland deposits (Pleistocene)**— Remnant deposits formed by paleo-springs and wetlands. Deposit is calcareous silt and fine sand and forms dissected platform

Qigs   **Intermediate groundwater-discharge spring mound deposits (late and middle Pleistocene)**—Silt and fine sand in former zones of groundwater-discharge. Generally white to light brown; compact. Commonly forms light-colored, raised features with 1 to 2 m of relief

44

above surrounding landscape often in close association with Qygs deposits. Contains one or more pedogenic calcic horizon, stage III to IV. Little vegetation, generally dissected. Exposures are present within west-flowing axial-valley drainage north of the Pisgah basalt flow near Hector and are closely associated with Quaternary fault exposures

LACUSTRINE DEPOSITS

Qil   **Intermediate lacustrine deposits (late and middle Pleistocene)**—Pluvial lake deposits including weakly to moderately indurated clay, silt, sandy silt, fine to coarse sand, rounded beach gravel, and pebbly to cobbly distal fan and (or) deltaic deposits. Lacustrine deposits along and near the Mojave River, from near Manix Wash to the northern border of the map area, were named the Manix formation by Jefferson and Reynolds (1985) and Jefferson (2003). We locally divide these deposits into several litho-facies:

Qilc   **Coarse lacustrine-alluvial sediment**—Fine sand to pebbly or cobbly coarse sand

Qilf   **Fine lacustrine sediment**—Clay to sandy silt

Qilg   **Lacustrine beach gravel**—Rounded gravel and gravelly sand

Qils   **Lacustrine sand**—Well sorted

EROSIONAL SURFACES AND HILLSLOPE DEPOSITS

HILLSLOPE DEPOSITS

Hillslopes deposits are bare rock or thin deposits, generally <2 m, underlain by rock. Deposits consist of zones of mechanically and chemically weathered rock or materials transported short distances by gravity and flowing water. They cover mountainous regions where slopes are steep (usually >3° degrees), significant sediment has not accumulated, and bedrock typically crops out. Thicker, aerially consistent units were distinguished as colluvium.

Qha   **Abundant hillslope deposits (Holocene and Pleistocenc)** Miscellaneous poorly dated hillslope materials (colluvium, talus, regolith, and landslide deposits) that are generally <2 m thick but cover more than half of the land surface. Patchy bedrock outcrops are exposed in remainder of area

Qhs   **Sparse hillslope deposits (Holocene and Pleistocene)**—Miscellaneous poorly dated hillslope materials (colluvium, talus, regolith, and landslide deposits) that are generally <2 m thick but cover less than half of the land surface. Patchy bedrock outcrops are exposed in remainder of area

MASS-WASTING COLLUVIAL DEPOSITS

Qymc   **Young colluvial deposits (Holocene and latest Pleistocene)**—Poorly sorted, muddy sand and gravel containing clasts as large as boulders, derived from nearby areas upslope, that are typically angular and massive to very poorly bedded. Loose to moderately compact colluvial materials thicker than 2 m covering a wide area; exact age undetermined. Poor to moderate soil development, generally increasing with abundance of fine-grained sediment. Landforms range from steep talus slopes to concave-up colluvial aprons that grade into alluvial fans

Qimc   **Intermediate colluvial deposits (late and middle Pleistocene)**—Poorly sorted, muddy sand and gravel containing clasts as large as boulders, derived from nearby areas upslope, typically angular and massive to very poorly bedded. Loose to moderately compact colluvial materials thicker than 2 m covering a wide area; exact age undetermined. Generally smooth deposit surfaces that are sharply incised by gullies. Exposed clasts either darkened by desert varnish or moderately to deeply etched, depending on lithology. Soil may have A_v horizons as much as 5 cm thick and moderate to strong reddening near top of B horizon. B_t horizon tends to be well developed, but calcic accumulation is unevenly developed and generally does not exceed stage II to III, thus is typically less developed than calcic horizons in alluvial deposits of similar age. Soil development appears to be greatest where original deposit contains abundant silt and clay. Detrital composition reflects that of rocks and sediments lying directly uphill. In some areas, deposits form steep slopes covered by darkly varnished boulders

PEDIMENT SURFACES

Gently sloping erosion surfaces and associated alluvial veneers in various stages of incision. Generally more planar than hillslope surfaces and less steeply inclined, mostly sloping a few degrees. Generally forms in felsic plutonic rocks that weather to grus (fpg) and in partly consolidated sediments (pc). Substrate designations follow hyphen (-) in unit symbol. Good examples of pediments are present in the upper parts of eastern Stoddard Valley near the Ord Mountains. Divided into three units distinguished by different degrees of dissection:

Qpv   **Veneered pediments**—Minimally incised surfaces having extensive alluvial veneers

Qpi   **Incised pediments**—Moderately incised surfaces having only sparse, patchy alluvial veneers; alluvial deposits mainly restricted to incised channels

Qpd   **Deeply dissected pediments**—Deeply dissected surfaces represented by accordant summits of bedrock pinnacles. Eroded bedrock between pinnacles may be exposed or covered by alluvial deposits

QUATERNARY AND LATE TERTIARY VOLCANIC ROCKS

Descriptions for Pisgah and Sunshine craters summarized from Wise (1966).

Qv   **Volcanic rocks (Quaternary)**—Lava flows and cinder cones of basaltic composition. Consists mainly of lava flows and subordinate cinder cones. Flow in northern Rodman Mountains dated at about 750 ka (M. Oskin, written commun., 2009)

    Volcanic rocks of Pisgah crater (latest Pleistocene)—Flows and cinder cones of olivine basalt

Qvp1   **First eruptive phase**—Microporphyritic alkali-olivine basalt with rare olivine phenocrysts (< 2mm)

46

Qvp2	**Second eruptive phase**—Second eruptive phase. Porphyritic basalt with olivine (2–3 mm) and plagioclase (2–5 mm) phenocrysts; mostly aa flows, with some pahoehoe
Qvp3	**Final eruptive phase**—Final eruptive phase. Porphyritic basalt containing plagioclase phenocrysts larger than 10 mm and clustered olivine phenocrysts 5–6 mm in diameter. Pahoehoe flows
Qvpc	**Cinders**— Cinders forming rim and slopes of Pisgah crater

Sunshine crater (Pleistocene)—Alkali-olivine basalt flows

Qvss	**Sunshine Cone flows**— Alkali-olivine basalt with olivine phenocrysts (3–5 mm) and occasional plagioclase phenocrysts
Qvsl	**Lavic flows**— Porphyritic alkali-olivine basalt with phenocrysts of olivine and plagioclase; distinguished from other flows in the region by presence of sparse titanaugite phenocrysts
QTv	**Lava flows (early Pleistocene to late Pliocene)**—Lava flows thought to be late Tertiary or early Quaternary in age based on degree of surface weathering

SUBSTRATE MATERIALS (PRE-QUATERNARY)

Bedrock substrate materials Shallowly buried bedrock and partly consolidated sedimentary materials that underlie surficial deposits and pediment and hillslope veneers. Ages range from Pliocene to early Proterozoic. Bedrock data come from several sources, primarily Dibblee (1966, 1967a,b), Dibblee and Bassett (1966a,b), and Bassett and Kupfer (1964). The following rock types are subdivided by mode of origin, chemical composition, and weathering products:

pc	**Partly consolidated sediments**—Moderately to weakly consolidated sedimentary deposits; locally includes volcanic rocks or highly altered rocks. Typically Tertiary in age. May form badland topography. Weathering products include silt and clay. May be mapped as QToa where possibly includes Pleistocene deposits
mv	**Intermediate to mafic volcanic rocks**—Volcanic rocks generally containing <68% SiO_2, such as andesite and basalt. Includes flows and ejecta. Weathering products include clay. Alluvial fans derived from mafic volcanic rocks typically contain abundant boulders
fv	**Felsic volcanic rocks**—Volcanic rocks generally containing >68% SiO_2, such as rhyolite, rhyodacite, dacite, and felsite. Includes flows and ejecta. Weathered materials include quartz, feldspar, and clay
mp	**Intermediate to mafic plutonic rocks**—Plutonic rocks generally containing < 68% SiO_2, such as gabbro, diorite, monzodiorite, syenite, and alkalic rocks. Weathered materials primarily feldspars, amphiboles, and micas
fp	**Felsic plutonic rocks**—Plutonic rocks generally containing >68% SiO_2, including granite and granodiorite
fpg	**Felsic plutonic rocks that weather to grus**—Plutonic rocks that generally contain >68% SiO_2 and readily distinguished by mechanical weathering, yielding granules and sand of feldspar and quartz. Mainly consists of Cretaceous granite and granodiorite

47

sl   **Siliciclastic rocks**—Silicic sedimentary and metamorphic rocks, such as quartz-rich sandstone, shale, siltstone, and quartzite. Weathering products commonly include quartz, silt, and clay

mr   **Metamorphic rocks**—Metamorphic rocks of complexly mixed lithology, such as gneiss, migmatite, and structurally mixed rocks. Weathered materials variable

ca   **Carbonate rocks**—Sedimentary and metasedimentary rocks composed of carbonates of calcium and magnesium; includes marble, dolomite, and limestone. Commonly weathers to form silt-rich detritus

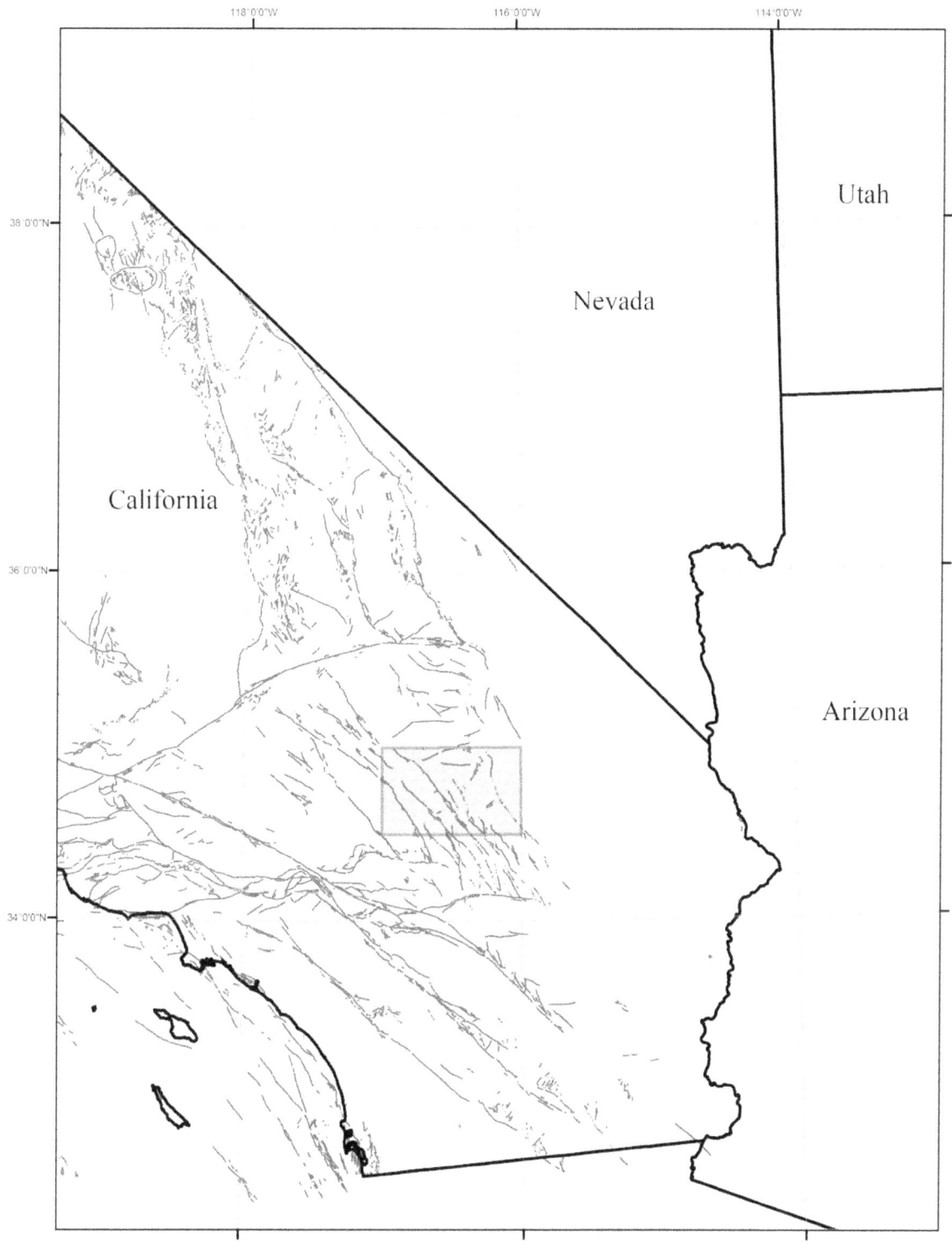

Figure 1. Location of the Newberry Springs quadrangle (gray box) in southern California. Faults (purple lines) from Jennings (1977).

Figure 2. Location of features in the Newbery Springs quadrangle. Shaded-relief map extracted from the National Elevation Dataset (NED). Road network extracted from ESRI USA Streen map.

50

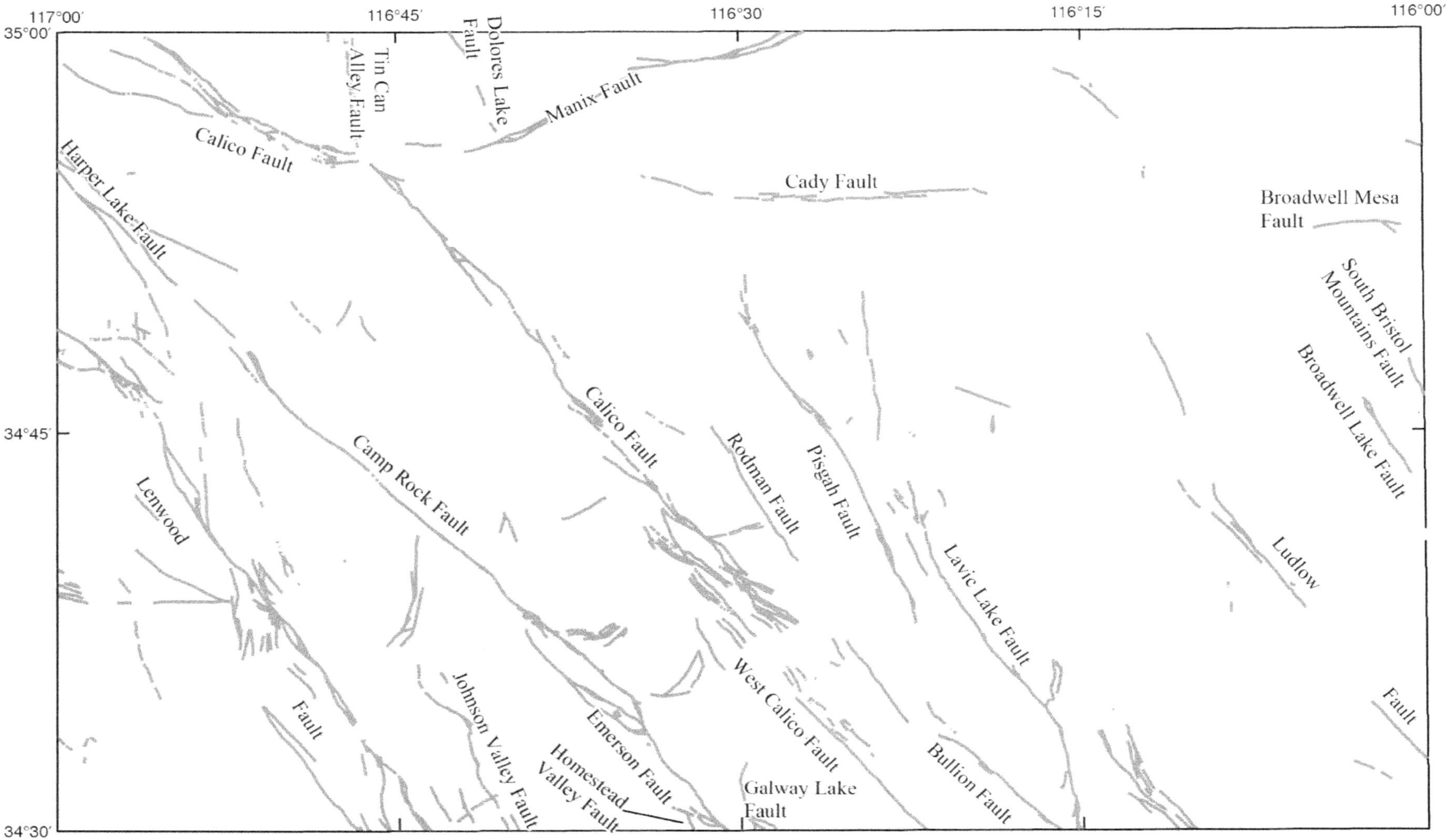

Figure 3. Quaternary faults (red lines) of the Newberry Springs quadrangle.

51

Figure 4.   Ludlow Fault. Top: evening view looking southwest from Route 66, showing truncated late Tertiary to early Quaternary sediments that form a prominent mid-fan scarp. Bottom: outcrop near the gas line road south of Ludlow where the fault truncates a Quaternary Bt horizon against older partially consolidated sediments (shovel is next to fault).

Figure 5. Lavic Lake playa ruptures in 2005. Top left: rupture showing sink holes and vegetation along fracture, view facing south. Top right: nearby rupture shows greater sediment infill and established vegetation, view facing north. Bottom right: playa fringe rupture just south of outcropping basalt; rupture is difficult to distinguish, coinciding with anomalous vegetated hummocky topography. Bottom left: rupture in desert pavement; Bt horizon is exposed and eroding; basalt clasts are derived from nearby flow, view facing north.

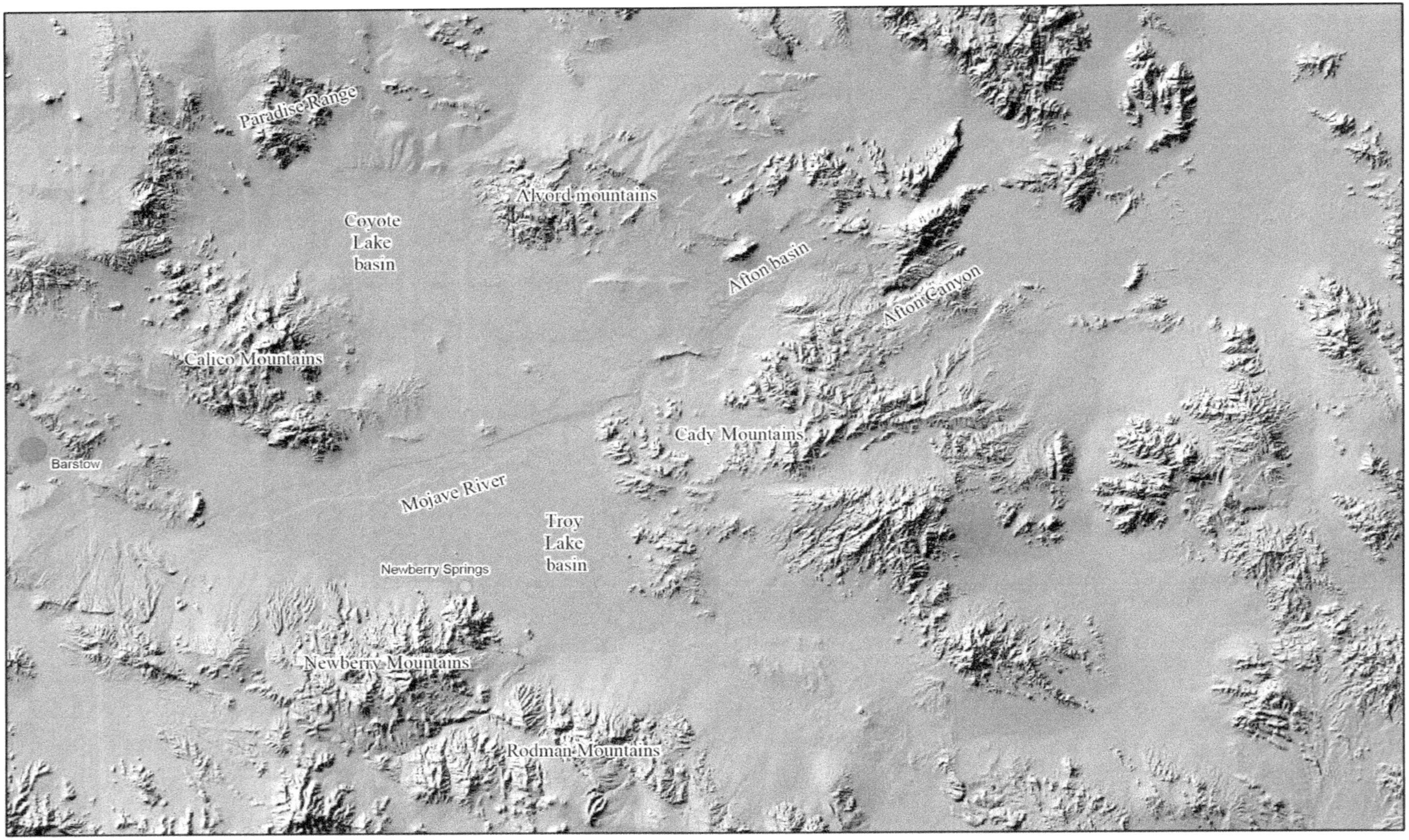

Figure 6. Approximate location of Lake manix (orange) at the highstand of 543 meters (based on modern topography).

54

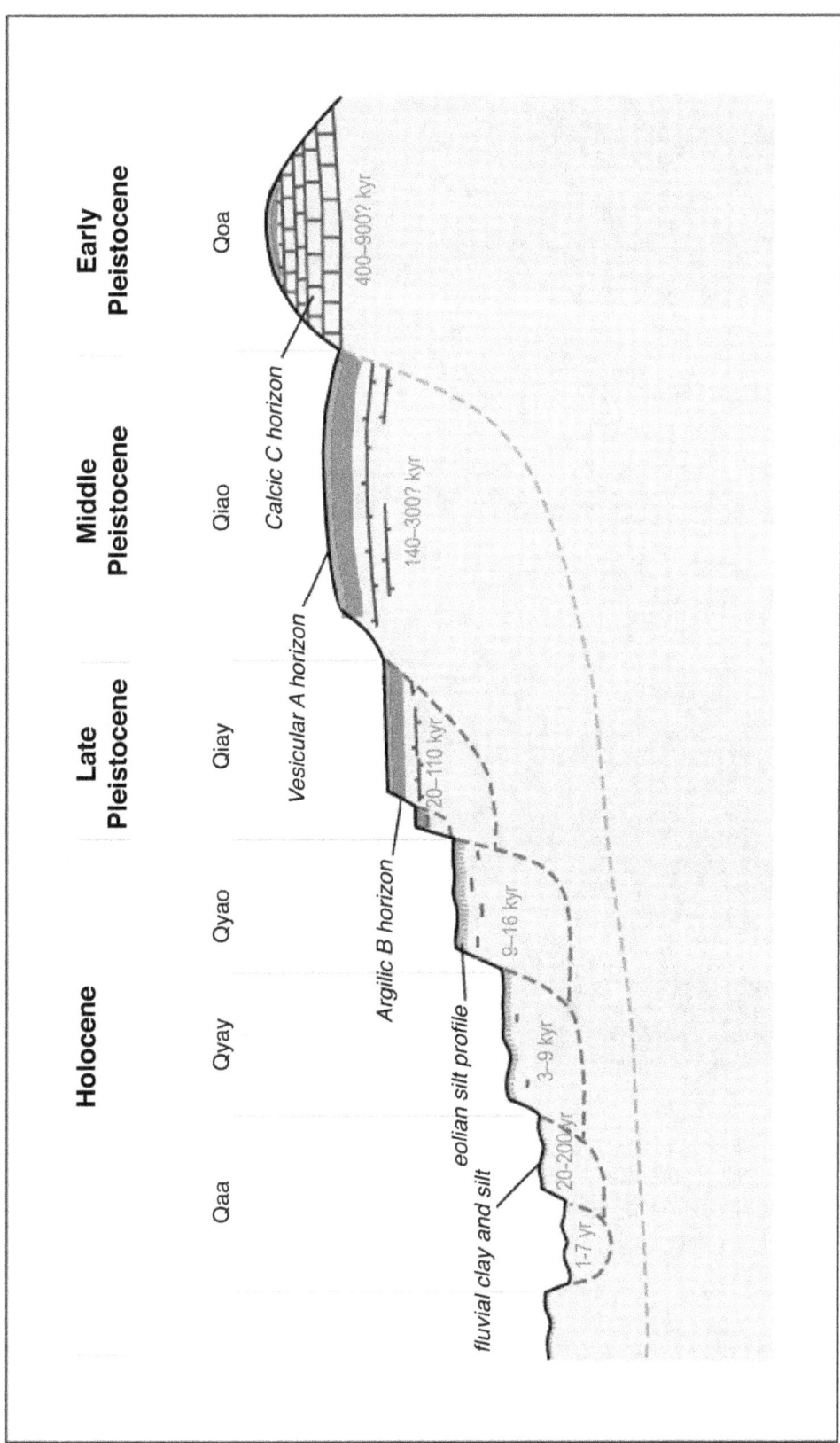

Figure 7. Conceptual model of the relation of soil development, inset surfaces, and age (modified from Miller and others, 2009).

55

Figure 8. Photographs of well-developed desert pavement on unit Qiao, northeastern Cady Mountains. Top: view facing east; note lack of perennial plants, flatness of surface, and large clasts that project higher than the pavement surface. Bottom: vertical view showing interlocking, poorly to moderately sorted, sub-angular, varnished clasts inset firmly into the underlying Av horizon.

Figure 9. Developing desert pavement, unvarnished, on unit Qyao. Top: landscape photo shows the presence of perennials and somewhat flat surface. Bottom: vertical view showing weakly varnished, interlocking pavement stones.

Figure 10.   Moderately developed desert pavement associated with eolian sand-rich alluvium, on unit Qiaey, northeastern Cady Mountains; clasts tend to be non-interlocking, with poor to moderate varnish, and appear to float on a sandy Av horizon.

Figure 11. Broken glass incorporated into desert pavement on unit Qiao, northeastern Cady Mountains. Top: oblique view. Bottom: vertical closeup; glass shards have all or part of their convex underside embedded in the underlying Av horizon.

Figure 12. Two views of "ripples" in desert pavement, unit Qiay. Top: view downhill across a desert pavement, Cady Mountains; pavement has lighter-colored transverse bars or "ripples" oriented approximately perpendicular to the maximum slope. Bottom: Nearly vertical close-up of pavement in eastern Cady Mountains; bars are composed of very fine gravel and sand overlying, and sometimes exposing, the underlying Av horizon.

Figure 13. Desert pavement on unit Qiwey in large wash north of Ludlow. Eolian influx apparently inhibits formation of clast cover with tight interlocking fabric.

References Cited

Anderson, K.C., 1999, Processes of vesicular horizon development and desert pavement formation on basalt flows of the Cima volcanic field and alluvial fans of the Avawatz Mountains piedmont, Mojave Desert, California: Doctoral Thesis, University of California, Riverside, 191 p.

Atwater, T., 1992, Constraints from plate reconstructions for Cenozoic tectonic regimes of southern and eastern California: San Bernardino County Museum Association Special Publication, v. 92–1, p. 1–2.

Bassett, A.M., and Kupfer, D.H., 1964, A geologic reconnaissance in the southeastern Mojave Desert, California: California Division of Mines and Geology Special Report 83, 43 p.

Bedford, D.R., Miller, D.M., and Phelps, G.A., 2006, Preliminary surficial geologic map database of the Amboy 30 x 60 minute quadrangle, California: U.S. Geological Survey Open-File Report 2006–1165, scale 1:100,000.

Bezore, S., and Pridmore, C., 1999, Extended Miocene rocks of the Box Canyon area, San Bernardino County, California: San Bernardino County Museum Association Quarterly, v. 63, no. 3, p. 95–99.

Bishop, C.C., 1963, Geologic map of California, Olaf P. Jenkins edition; needles sheet: California Division of Mines and Geology, scale 1:250,000.

Brady, R.H., III, 1992, The Eastern California shear zone in the northern Bristol Mountains, southeastern California: San Bernardino County Museum Association Special Publication, v. 92–1, p. 6–10.

Buwalda, J.P., 1914, Pleistocene beds at Manix in the eastern Mojave Desert region: Bulletin, Department of Geology, Berkeley, University of California, v. 7, no. 24, p. 443–464.

Buwalda, J.P., and Richter, C.F., 1948, Movement on the Manix (California) fault on April 10, 1947: Geological Society of America Bulletin, v. 59, no. 12, Part 2, p. 1367.

Carter, J.N., Luyendyk, B.P., and Terres, R.R., 1987, Neogene clockwise tectonic rotation of the eastern Transverse Ranges, California, suggested by paleomagnetic vectors: Geological Society of America Bulletin, v. 98, no. 2, p. 199–206.

Casey, B.J., 1981, The geology of a portion of the northeastern Bristol Mountains, Mojave Desert, California: Master's Thesis, University of California, Riverside.

Cooke, R.U., 1970, Stone pavements in deserts: Annals of the Association of American Geographers, v. 60, p. 560–577.

Cox, B.F., in press, Stratigraphy and structure of the Newberry Mountains, Southern California, and implications for tectonic evolution of the Mojave Desert Province: U.S. Geological Survey Professional Paper xxxx.

Cox, B.F., Griscom, A., Kilburn, J.E., Raines, G.L., Knepper, D.H., Jr., Sabine, C., and Kuizon, L., 1987, Mineral resources of the Newberry Mountains and Rodman Mountains Wilderness Study Areas, San Bernardino County, California: U.S. Geological Survey Bulletin 1712–A, 28 p.

Cox, B.F., and Wilshire, H.G., 1993, Geologic map of the area around the Nebo Annex, Marine Corps Logistics Base, Barstow, California: U.S. Geological Survey Open-File Report 93–0568, 36 p., scale 1:12,000.

Cox, B.F., and Wilshire, H.G., 1994, Geologic map of the Yermo Annex and vicinity, Marine Corps Logistics Base, Barstow, California: U.S. Geological Survey Open-File Report 94–0681, scale 1:12,000.

Densmore, J.N., Cox, B.F., and Crawford, S.M., 1997, Geohydrology and water quality of Marine Corps Logistics Base, Nebo and Yermo Annexes, near Barstow, California: U.S. Geological Survey Water-Resources Investigations Report 96–4301, 116 p.

Dibblee, T.W., Jr., 1964a, Geologic map of the Ord Mountains quadrangle, San Bernardino County, California: U.S. Geological Survey Miscellaneous Geologic Investigations Map I–427, scale 1:62,500.

Dibblee, T.W., Jr., 1964b, Geological map of the Rodman Mountains quadrangle, San Bernardino County, California: U.S. Geological Survey Miscellaneous Geologic Investigations Map I–430, scale 1:62,500.

Dibblee, T.W., Jr., 1966, Geologic map of the Lavic quadrangle, San Bernardino County, California: U.S. Geological Survey Miscellaneous Geologic Investigations Map I–472, scale 1:62,500.

Dibblee, T.W., Jr., 1967a, Geologic map of the Broadwell Lake quadrangle, San Bernardino County, California: U.S. Geological Survey Miscellaneous Geologic Investigations Map I–478, scale 1:62,500.

Dibblee, T.W., Jr., 1967b, Geologic map of the Ludlow quadrangle, San Bernardino County, California: U.S. Geological Survey Miscellaneous Geologic Investigations Map I–477, scale 1:62,500.

Dibblee, T.W., Jr., 1970, Geologic map of the Daggett quadrangle, San Bernardino County, California: U.S. Geological Survey Miscellaneous Geologic Investigations Map I–492, scale 1:62,500.

Dibblee, T.W., Jr., and Bassett, A.M., 1966a, Geologic map of the Cady Mountains quadrangle, San Bernardino County, California: U.S. Geological Survey Miscellaneous Geologic Investigations Map I–467, scale 1:62,500.

Dibblee, T.W., Jr., and Bassett, A.M., 1966b, Geologic map of the Newberry quadrangle, San Bernardino County, California: U.S. Geological Survey Miscellaneous Geologic Investigations Map I–461, scale 1:62,500.

Dokka, R.K., 1983, Displacements on late Cenozoic strike-slip faults of the central Mojave Desert, California: Geology, v. 11, no. 5, p. 305–308.

Dokka, R.K., and Travis, C.J., 1990, Late Cenozoic strike-slip faulting in the Mojave Desert, California: Tectonics, v. 9, no. 2, p. 311–340.

Dudash, S.L., 2006, Preliminary surficial geologic map of a Calico Mountains piedmont and part of Coyote Lake, Mojave Desert, San Bernardino County, California: U.S. Geological Survey Open-File Report 2006–1090, scale 1:24,000.

EMCON Associates, 1993, Dessication features investigation: Emcon Associates, Broadwell Basin specified hazardous waste facility final environmental impact report/environmental impact statement BLM-CA-PT-91-022-1793, v. 2, 56 p.

Engel, C.G., and Sharp, R.P., 1956, Chemical data on desert varnish: Bulletin of the Geological Society of America, v. 69, no. 5, p. 487–518.

Enzel, Y., Wells, S.G., and Lancaster, N., 2003, Late Pleistocene lakes along the Mojave River, Southeast California, Special Paper: Geological Society of America, v. 368, p. 61–77.

Ford, J.P., Dokka, R.K., Crippen, R.E., and Blom, R.G., 1990, Faults in the Mojave Desert, California, as revealed on enhanced Landsat images: Science, v. 248, no. 4958, p. 1000–1003.

Forester, R.M., Miller, D.M., and Pedone, V.A., 2002, Ground water and ground-water discharge carbonate deposits in warm deserts, *in* Reynolds, R.E., ed., Land of Lost Lakes: 2003 Desert Symposium, Fullerton, California State University, p. 27–36.

Gardner, D.L., 1940, Geology of the Newberry and Ord Mountains, San Bernardino County, California, California Journal of Mines and Geology, v. 36, no. 3, p. 257–292.

Garfunkel, Z., 1974, Model for the Late Cenozoic tectonic history of the Mojave Desert, California, and for its relation to adjacent regions: Geological Society of America Bulletin, v. 85, no. 12, p. 1931–1944.

Gile, L.H., Peterson, F.F., and Grossman, R.B., 1966, Morphological and genetic sequences of carbonate accumulations in desert soils: Soil Science, v. 101, no. 5, p. 347–360.

Glazner, A.F., Bartley, J.M., and Sanner, W.K., 2000, Nature of the southwestern boundary of the central Mojave Tertiary province, Rodman Mountains, California: Geological Society of America Bulletin, v. 112, no. 1, p. 34–44.

Glazner, A.F., Walker, J.D., Bartley, J.M., and Fletcher, J.M., 2002, Cenozoic evolution of the Mojave Block of Southern California: Geological Society of America Memoir, v. 195, p. 19–41.

Groat, C.G., 1967, Geology and hydrology of the Troy playa area, San Bernardino County, California: University of Massachusetts, M.S. Thesis, 133 p.

Hagar, D.J., 1966, Geomorphology of Coyote Valley, San Bernardino County, California: University of Massachusetts, M.S. Thesis, 210 p.

Hart, E.W., Bryant, W.A., and Treiman, J.A., 1993, Surface faulting associated with the June 1992 Landers earthquake, California: California Geology, v. 46, no. 1, p. 10–16.

Hawkins, H.G., 1976, Strike slip displacement along the Camp Rock fault, central Mojave Desert, San Bernardino, California: Unpub. M.S. Thesis, University of Southern California, 63 p.

Hill, R.L., and Beeby, D.J., 1977, Surface faulting associated with the 5.2 magnitude Galway Lake earthquake of May 31, 1975, Mojave Desert, San Bernardino County, California: Geological Society of America Bulletin, v. 88, no. 10, p. 1378–1384.

Howard, K.H., and Miller, D.M., 1992, Late Cenozoic faulting at the boundary between the Mojave and Sonoran blocks, Bristol Lake area, California: San Bernardino County Museum Association Special Publication, v. 92–1, p. 37–47.

Irvine, P.J., and Hill, R.L., 1993, Surface rupture along a portion of the Emerson Fault, California Geology, v. 46, no. 1, p. 23–26.

Jachens, R.C., Langenheim, V.E., and Matti, J.C., 2002, Relationship of the 1999 Hector Mine and 1992 Landers Fault ruptures to offsets on Neogene faults and distribution of late Cenozoic basins in the eastern California shear zone: Bulletin of the Seismological Society of America, v. 92, no. 4, p. 1592–1605.

Jefferson, G.T., 2003, Stratigraphy and Paleontology of the middle to late Pleistocene Manix formation, and paleoenvironments of the central Mojave River, southern California, *in* Yehouda, E., Wells, S.G., and Lancaster, N., eds., Paleoenvironments and paleohydrology of the Mojave and southern Great Basin Deserts: Geological Society of America Special Paper 368, p. 43–60.

Jefferson, G.T., and Reynolds, R.E., 1985, Stratigraphy and geologic history of the Pleistocene Lake Manix formation, central Mojave Desert, California, *in* Geologic investigations along interstate 15; Cajon Pass to manix Lake, California: San Bernardino County Museum Association Special Publication, Redlands, CA, p. 157–169.

Jennings, C.W., 1994, Fault activity map of California and adjacent areas: California Department of Conservation, Division of Mines and Geology California Geologic Data Map Series Map 6, scale 1:750,000.

Jenny, H., 1941, Factors of soil formation—a system of quantitative pedology: Dover Publications, New York, 191 pp.

Keaton, J.R., and Keaton, R.T., 1977, Manix Fault Zone, San Bernardino County, California: California Geology, v. 30, no. 8, p. 177–186.

Kupfer, D.H., and Bassett, A.M., 1962, Geologic reconnaissance map of part of the southeastern Mojave Desert, California: U.S. Geological Survey Miscellaneous Field Investigations MF–205, scale 1:125,000.

Liu, T., 2003, Blind testing of rock varnish microstratigraphy as a chronometric indicator; results on late Quaternary lava flows in the Mojave Desert, California: Geomorphology, v. 53, no. 3–4, p. 209–234.

Machette, M.N., 1985, Calcic soils of the southwestern United States, Weide, David L., ed., *in* Soils and Quaternary geology of the southwestern United States: Geological Society of America Special Paper 203, p. 1–22.

Machette, M.N., 2008, Terrestrial cosmogenic-nuclide dating of alluvial fans in Death Valley, California: U.S. Geological Survey Professional Paper1755, 44 p.

Mahan, S.A., Miller, D.M., Menges, C.M., and Yount, J.C., 2007, Late Quaternary stratigraphy and luminescence geochronology of the northeastern Mojave Desert: Quaternary International, v. 166, no. 1, p. 61–78.

McCulloh, T.H., 1965, Geologic map of the Nebo and Yermo quadrangles, San Bernardino County, California: U.S. Geological Survey Open-File Report 65–107, Scale 1:24,000.

McFadden, L.D., McDonald, E.V., Wells, S.G., Anderson, K., Quade, J., and Forman, S.L., 1998, The vesicular layer and carbonate collars of desert soils and pavements; formation, age and relation to climate change: Geomorphology, v. 24, no. 2–3, p. 101–145.

McFadden, L.D., Wells, S.G., Dohrenwend, J.C., and Turrin, B.D., 1983, A chronosequence of cumulic soils formed in eolian parent materials on flows of the late Cenozoic Cima volcanic field, Mojave Desert, California: Geological Society of America, Abstracts with Programs, v. 15, no. 5, p. 422.

McFadden, L.D., Wells, S.G., Dohrenwend, J.C., and Turrin, B.D., 1984, Cumulic soils formed in eolian parent materials on flows of the Cima volcanic field, Mojave Desert, California: Geological Society of America Fieldtrip Guide book, Western Geological Excursions, v. 1, p. 208–221.

McGill, S.F., Murray, B.C., Maher, K.A., Lieske, J.H., Jr., and Rowan, L.R., 1988, Quaternary history of the Manix Fault, Lake Manix Basin, Mojave Desert, California: Quarterly of San Bernardino County Museum Association, v. 35, no. 3–4, p. 3–20.

McGill, S.F., and Rubin, C.M., 1999, Surficial slip distribution on the central Emerson Fault during the June 28, 1992, Landers earthquake, California: Journal of Geophysical Research, v. 104, no. B3, p. 4811–4833.

McKenzie, D., and Jackson, J., 1983, The relationship between strain rates, crustal thickening, palaeomagnetism, finite strain and fault movements within a deforming zone: Earth and Planetary Science Letters, v. 65, no. 1, p. 182–202.

Meek, N., 1990, Late Quaternary geochronology and geomorphology of the Manix basin, San Bernardino County, California: University of California Los Angeles, Ph.D., 212 p.

Meek, N., 1994, The stratigraphy and geomorphology of Coyote Basin, central Mojave Desert, California: Quarterly of the San Bernardino County Museum Association, v. 41, no. 3, p. 5–13.

Meek, N., 1999, New discoveries about the late Wisconsin of the Mojave river system: San Bernardino County Museum Association Quarterly, v. 46, no. 3, p. 113–118.

Meek, N., and Battles, D.A., 1991, Displacement along the Manix Fault: California Geology, v. 44, no. 2, p. 33–38.

Messina, P., Stoffer, P., and Smith, W.C., 2005, Macropolygon morphology, development, and classification on North Panamint and Eureka Playas, Death Valley National Park, California: Earth-Science Reviews, v. 73, no. 1–4, p. 309–322.

Miller, D.M., Bedford, D.R., Hughson, D.L., McDonald, E.V., Robinson, S.E., and Schmidt, K.M., 2009, Mapping Mojave Desert ecosystem properties with surficial geology, in Webb, R.H., Fenstermaker, L.F., Heaton, J.S., Hughson, D.L., McDonald, E.V., and Miller, D.M., eds., The Mojave Desert—Ecosystem Processes and Sustainability: Reno, University of Nevada Press, 27 p.

Miller, D.M., Dudash, S.L., Green, H.L., Lidke, D.J., Amoroso, L., Phelps, G.A., and Schmidt, K.M., 2007, A new Quaternary view of northern Mojave Desert tectonics suggests changing fault patterns during the late Pleistocene, in Miller, D.M., and Valin, Z.C., eds., Geomorphology and tectonics at the intersection of Silurian and Death Valleys, southern California: U.S. Geological Survey Open-File Report 2007–1424, p. 157–171.

Miller, D.M., Howard, K.A., and John, B.E., 1982, Preliminary geology of the Bristol Lake region, Mojave Desert, California: Geological Society of America, Cordilleran Section 78th Annual Meeting, p. 91–100.

Miller, D.M., Miller, R.J., Nielson, J.E., Wilshire, H.G., Howard, K.A., and Stone, P., 1991, Preliminary geologic map of the East Mojave National Scenic Area, California: U.S. Geological Survey Open-File Report 91-435, scale 1:100,000.

Nagy, E.A., and Murray, B.C., 1991, Stratigraphy and intra-basin correlation of the Mojave River formation, central Mojave Desert, California: Quarterly of the San Bernardino County Museum Association, v. 38, no. 2, p. 5–30.

Nagy, E.A., and Murray, B., 1996, Plio-Pleistocene deposits adjacent to the Manix Fault; implications for the history of the Mojave River and Transverse Ranges uplift: Sedimentary Geology, v. 103, no. 1–2, p. 9–21.

Neal, J.T., 1968, Playa surface morphology; miscellaneous investigations: Office of Aerospace Research, U.S. Air Force AFCRL-68-0133, 150 p.

Neal, J.T., Langer, A.M., and Kerr, P.F., 1968, Giant desiccation polygons of Great Basin playas: Geological Society of America Bulletin, v. 79, no. 1, p. 69–90.

Oskin, M., and Iriondo, A., 2004, Large-magnitude transient strain accumulation on the Blackwater Fault, Eastern California shear zone: Geology, v. 32, no. 4, p. 313–316.

Oskin, M., Perg, L., Blumentritt, D., Mukhopadhyay, S., and Iriondo, A., 2007, Slip rate of the Calico fault; Implications for geologic versus geodetic rate discrepancy in the Eastern California Shear Zone: Journal of Geophysical Research, v. 112, B03402, 16 p.

Padgett, D.C., and Rockwell, T.K., 1994, Paleoseismology of the Lenwood Fault, San Bernardino County, California: South Coast Geological Society Annual Field Trip Guidebook, v. 22, p. 222–237.

Peterson, F.F., 1981, Landforms of the Basin and Range province defined for soil survey: Nevada Agricultural Experiment Station Technical Bulletin, no. 28, 52 p.

Phillips, F.M., 2003, Cosmogenic (super 36) Cl ages of Quaternary basalt flows in the Mojave Desert, California, USA: Geomorphology, v. 53, no. 3–4, p. 199–208.

Pluhar, C.J., Kirschvink, J.L., and Adams, R.W., 1991, Magnetostratigraphy and clockwise rotation of the Plio-Pleistocene Mojave River formation, central Mojave Desert, California, Quarterly of San Bernardino County Museum Association, v. 38, no. 2, p. 31–42.

Quade, J., Forester, R.M., and Whelan, J.F., 2003, Late Quaternary paleohydrologic and paleotemperature change in southern Nevada: Geological Society of America Special Paper 368, p. 165–188.

Quade, J., Mifflin, M.D., Pratt, W.L., McCoy, W., and Burckle, L., 1995, Fossil spring deposits in the southern Great Basin and their implications for changes in water-table levels near Yucca Mountain, Nevada, during Quaternary time: Geological Society of America Bulletin, v. 107, no. 2, p. 213–230.

Rasmussen and Associates, 1990, Geologic and Geotechnical feasibility investigation, proposed residuals repository, Broadwell dry lake, north of Ludlow, California: San Bernardino, California, Gary S. Rasmussen and Associates, project no. 2604.3, 89 p.

Reheis, M.C., Goodmacher, J.C., Harden, J.W., McFadden, L.D., Rockwell, T.K., Shroba, R.R., Sowers, J.M., and Taylor, E.M., 1995, Quaternary soils and dust deposition in southern Nevada and California, Geological Society of America Bulletin, v. 107, no. 9, 1003–1022 p.

Reheis, M.C., Harden, J.W., McFadden, T.K., Shroba, R.R., 1989, Development Rates of Late Quaternary soils, Silver Lake Playa, California: Soil Science Society of America Journal, v. 53, p. 1127–1140.

Reynolds, R.L., Reheis, M.C., Neff, J.C., Goldstein, H., and Yount, J., 2006, Late Quaternary eolian dust in surficial deposits of a Colorado Plateau grassland; controls on distribution and ecologic effects: Catena, v. 66, no. 3, 251–266 p.

Reynolds, R.E., and Reynolds, R.L., 1985, Late Pleistocene faunas from Daggett and Yermo, *in* Geologic investigations along interstate 15, Cajon Pass to manix Lake, California: San Bernardino County Museum, Redlands, CA, p. 175–191.

Richter, C.F., 1947, The Manix (California) earthquake of April 10, 1947: Seismological Society of America Bulletin, v. 37, p. 171–179.

Rogers, T.H. 1967. Geologic Map of California, San Bernardino Sheet: California Division of Mines and Geology, scale 1:250,000.

Ron, H., Beroza, G., and Nur, A., 2001, Simple model explains complex faulting, Eos, Transactions, American Geophysical Union, v. 82, no. 10, p. 125, 128–129.

Ross, T.M., 1992, Geologic and paleomagnetic constraints on the timing of initiation and amount of slip on the Rodman and Pisgah faults, central Mojave Desert, California: San Bernardino County Museum Association Special Publication, v. 92–1, p. 75–77.

Rubin, C.M., and Sieh, K., 1997, Long dormancy, low slip rate, and similar slipper-event for the Emerson Fault, eastern California shear zone: Journal of Geophysical Research, v. 102, no. B7, p. 15,319–15,333.

Rymer, M.J., Langenheim, V.E., and Hauksson, E., 2002, The Hector Mine, California, Earthquake of 16 October 1999: Introduction to the Special Issue Bulletin of the Seismological Society of America, v. 92, no. 4, p. 1147–1153.

Sharon, D., 1962, On the nature of hamadas in Israel: Zeitschrift fur Geomorphologie, v. 6, p. 129–147.

Sohn, M.F., Mahan, S.A., Knott, J.R., and Bowman, D.D., 2007, Luminescence ages for alluvial-fan deposits in southern Death Valley; implications for climate-driven sedimentation along a tectonically active mountain front: Quaternary International, v. 166, no. 1, p. 49–60.

Stoffer, P., 2004, Desert landforms and surface processes in the Mojave National Preserve and vicinity: U.S. Geological Survey Open-File Report 2004–1007, http://pubs.usgs.gov/of/2004/1007/intro.html.

Sylvester, A.G., Burmeister, K.C., and Wise, W.S., 2002, Faulting and effects of associated shaking at Pisgah Crater Volcano caused by the 16 October 1999 Hector Mine earthquake (M_w 7.1), central Mohave Desert, California: Bulletin of the Seismological Society of America, v. 92, no. 4, p. 1333–1340.

Thompson, D.G., 1929, The Mohave Desert region, California; geographic, geologic, and hydrographic reconnaissance: U.S. Geological Survey Water-Supply Paper W–0578, 759 p.

Treiman, J.A., Kendrick, K.J., Bryant, W.A., Rockwell, T.K., and McGill, S.F., 2002, Primary surface rupture associated with the M (sub w) 7.1 16 October 1999 Hector Mine earthquake, San Bernardino County, California: Bulletin of the Seismological Society of America, v. 92, no. 4, p. 1171–1191.

USGS and CGS, 2007, Quaternary fault and fold database for the United States: accessed September, 2007, at http//earthquakes.usgs.gov/regional/qfaults/.

Wells, S.G., Dohrenwend, J.C., McFadden, L.D., Turrin, B.D., and Mahrer, K.D., 1985, Late Cenozoic landscape evolution on lava flow surfaces of the Cima volcanic field, Mojave Desert, California: Geological Society of America Bulletin, v. 96, no. 12, p. 1518–1529.

Wells, S.G., McFadden, L.D., and Dohrenwend, J.C., 1987, Influence of late Quaternary climatic changes on geomorphic and pedogenic processes on a desert piedmont, eastern Mojave Desert, California: Quaternary Research, v. 27, no. 2, p. 130–146.

Wells, S.G., McFadden, L.D., Poths, J., and Olinger, C.T., 1995, Cosmogenic (super 3) He surface-exposure dating of stone pavements; implications for landscape evolution in deserts: Geology, v. 23, no. 7, p. 613–616.

Wise, W.S., 1968, Geologic map of the Pisgah and Sunshine Cone lava fields: NASA Technical letter, NASA–11, p. 8.